Ros Stephen

BOOK 2

Violinworks

A comprehensive method for the older beginner

MUSIC DEPARTMENT

OXFORD
UNIVERSITY PRESS

Great Clarendon Street, Oxford OX2 6DP,
United Kingdom

Oxford University Press is a department of the University of Oxford.
It furthers the University's objective of excellence in research, scholarship,
and education by publishing worldwide. Oxford is a registered trade mark of
Oxford University Press in the UK and in certain other countries

First published 2016

Impression: 1

ISBN 978-0-19-340269-0

Music and text origination by Julia Bovee
Text design by Adriana Sutton

Printed in Great Britain on acid-free paper by
Halstan & Co. Ltd, Amersham, Bucks.

Acknowledgements

Ros Stephen would like to thank: Julian Rowlands for writing piano accompaniments for many of the pieces in this book, and for modelling for the front cover photo; violinist Alison Gordon for modelling for the internal photos; Phil Croydon, Kathy Blackwell, and Jane Griffiths for their feedback and comments on the book; Robyn Elton and Jonathan Cunliffe for their extremely detailed editorial work; Marianne Haynes (violin), Triona Milne (viola), Laura Anstee (cello), Sarah Nicolls (piano), Jonathan Taylor (piano), Pete Rosser (accordion), Tom Mason (double bass), and Andrew Tween (drums), for their beautiful playing on the CD; and Ken Blair (engineer and co-producer) and Will Anderson for their work at the recording sessions and on the first stages of post-production.

CONTENTS

1 INTRODUCTION

WELCOME TO VIOLINWORKS Book 2! This book follows on from Book 1, introducing new notes for the left hand, vibrato, new bowing techniques, 3rd position, aural and technical exercises, improvisation, playing by ear, and a wide variety of music ranging from classical (Baroque, Classical, and Romantic) to jazz, world, and folk.

Website, CD, and piano accompaniments

As with Book 1, this method can be used with a teacher, but it is also designed to include all the information needed for self-learning, especially when used in conjunction with the website **www.violin-works.com**, which includes video demonstrations of many of the techniques described in the book—look out for the video icons. The website includes headings for each chapter, so it is easy to find what you're looking for. More information will be added as time goes on, so keep checking for updates and additional advice. Backing tracks for all pieces are also available on the website—practise playing along with piano, string quartet, or jazz or folk band!

The accompanying CD includes performance tracks (see the track numbers next to the icon). The repeats within pieces are generally not played on the CD, but the backing tracks on the website do contain repeats. It also includes printable PDFs of piano accompaniments for all pieces. PC users can access the PDFs by selecting 'Computer' from the start-up menu and right-clicking on the CD drive to open the CD. Mac users should double-click on the data disc that appears when the CD is inserted to see the PDF files.

The next two sections cover some key musical and technical points that you'll need to be aware of as you work through this book. Refer back to them regularly, especially as you learn new notes and finger positions.

Reminders and reference material

Left-hand fingering patterns

As described in Book 1, each finger of the left hand can adopt two basic positions, a semitone apart, known as 'high' and 'low' positions. The fingers are more extended in the high position and more upright and square in the low position. In this book you will learn to play in the low and high positions with all four fingers. Each new finger position gives rise to a new pattern of intervals between the fingers; we will use a shorthand such as 0--1--2--3-4 to describe the various different fingering patterns (or hand-shapes), where each dash represents a semitone.

Intonation

In this book, as in Book 1, you are encouraged to develop your ear in order to gain confidence in intonation (rather than relying on finger spacing charts or stickers on the fingerboard). Listen to the CD recordings, work through the aural exercises and, most importantly, sing or whistle your pieces and exercises before you play. If you can 'hear the notes in your head', you are much more likely to play in tune.

Intervals

You're already familiar with the concept of an interval as the distance between two notes, and you've encountered major, minor, and perfect intervals, as well as semitones and tones. In this book you'll come across two new types of interval: diminished and augmented. A diminished interval is a semitone smaller than a minor or perfect interval, and an augmented interval is a semitone larger than a major or perfect interval. The following intervals are referred to in this book (note that a minor 2nd is the same as a semitone, and the width of each interval increases by a semitone as you go up to the octave):

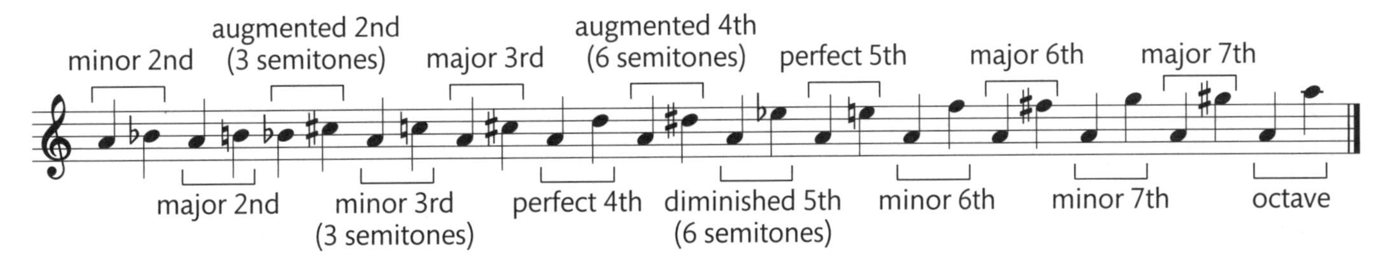

Key signatures and the circle of fifths

In Book 1 you learnt that a key signature dictates which sharps or flats to play in a piece of music. You also began to recognize the sound of major and minor intervals and chords, and understand the relationship between relative major and minor keys. As you learn more notes on the violin, and progress to more complex music, you'll expand your understanding of keys and the relationships between them, and you'll need to take note of the key signatures used in the pieces you're playing. The circle of fifths, which you'll find in the Appendix on page 100, gives an overview of all twelve key signatures. Use it to check the key of the piece you're working on, and to identify relative major and minor keys.

Practice tips and troubleshooting

As you begin to work on longer pieces, you may find some elements or passages more difficult than others. In these cases, try to isolate the section and focus your practice on the issue that needs troubleshooting, using the following tried and tested practice techniques.

Open-string bowing practice

If you've ever learnt the piano you'll be familiar with the concept of practising 'hands separately'. This is also important for the violin, particularly for the right hand.

Your bowing arm creates most of the expression in the music, so it's important to spend time thinking about how the bow is used in any musical phrase, for example how fast or slow it should be moved, which part of the bow to use, how to avoid running out of bow, how to avoid any unintended accents or bulges in the sound, etc. A good way to work on this is to practise the bowing on open strings without the left hand:

- Pick a short phrase that you'd like to work on and sing it a few times without your violin, while moving your right arm in the air as if bowing, for example the first four bars of 'Ellie's Jig' on page 8:

- Now play the phrase on a single open string using the same bow-strokes as you'd use when playing 'hands together'. This means any slurred notes will be played as a single, longer note. Make your playing sound alive and musical, with all the variations in tone colour, dynamic, and articulation that you'd like to hear when playing with both hands:

- Now work out which strings are used when playing 'hands together' and play the bowing pattern on the same open strings. This can require a bit of thought! Try to make your string crossings really smooth so that they don't disrupt the musical line:

- Now put the left-hand notes back in and notice the improvement!

Slow intonation practice

Slow practice is very important for the left hand as it gives you time to listen to your tuning and adjust if necessary.

- Pick a phrase that you'd like to work on and sing it a few times.
- Ignore the rhythm and any expressive markings and just play the notes with slow, even bow-strokes, listening very carefully to the intonation of each note.
- Where possible, check your intonation with open strings.
- Remember to listen out for 'ringing notes'—notes an octave above or below an open string sound very resonant when they are in tune because they cause the open string to vibrate at the same time (see Book 1, page 44).

Left-hand rhythms

Practising groups of even, quick notes, such as groups of four or more slurred quavers, with dotted rhythms can improve left-hand coordination and help make the left-hand fingers more rhythmic. For example, bar 6 of 'The Birdcatcher's Song' on page 11 could be practised like this:

Using 'preparation pauses'

To get a good, clear sound on the violin both the left-hand finger and the bow usually need to be in contact with the string fractionally before the bow begins to move. Squeaks and scratchy sounds are often caused by one or other hand not quite being ready to play. If you are finding a particular fingering or string-crossing problematic, pause for as long as you need to get your finger and bow in position on the string and play the note only when you're sure you're ready. Gradually make these 'preparation pauses' shorter until they're no longer there.

Practise with a metronome

Playing your pieces rhythmically and being in control of the tempo is one of the most important musical skills to learn. Tempos fluctuate in a natural-sounding musical performance, but this should be done in a thoughtful and controlled way. Common mistakes are to play hard bits more slowly than easy bits, and to rush fast notes. The easiest way to work on this is to practise regularly with a metronome.

- For fast passages: start at a slow tempo and gradually speed up the metronome until you can play perfectly in time at the performance tempo.
- For slow passages: practise at the performance tempo, counting the beats in your head along to the metronome so that you don't get lost when you switch it off!
- For passages with tricky rhythms, clap the rhythm while counting the beats out loud along to the metronome before playing.

When you can do this easily, turn off the metronome and allow yourself to play in a more natural and expressive way. Be aware that some styles of music require a stricter tempo than others. For example, rhythmic music such as jazz or folk usually requires a steady, consistent tempo, and classical music, particularly more romantic styles, tends to pull around more. Listening to lots of recordings will help with your interpretation. Practise exercises and scales with a metronome; metronome marks are suggested but choose a tempo that's comfortable for you.

2 NEW BOWING TECHNIQUES PART 1

Hooked bow-strokes in 6/8 time 

Hooked bow-strokes (pairs of uneven notes played in the same bow direction) are often used to join crotchet-quaver rhythms in faster 6/8 pieces such as jigs, giving the music a light and bouncy feel.

- Start at around the middle of the bow. Use about eight inches of bow for each pair of hooked notes at the slower tempo, and gradually make the bow-strokes shorter as you increase the speed.

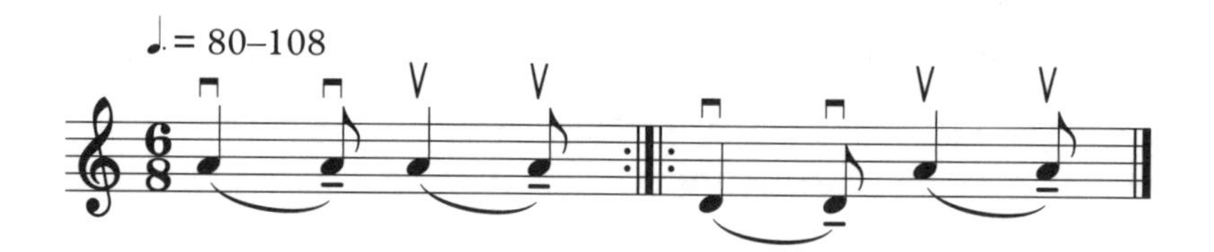

- Stop the bow lightly and briefly on the string at the end of each crotchet bow-stroke, keeping your right-hand fingers relaxed and flexible, then gently lean your 1st finger back down onto the bow stick to catch the string and start the hooked quaver with a clean, clear sound. Play changes in bow direction smoothly.
- Practise with a metronome set to a dotted crotchet beat. In your head, subdivide the beat into groups of three quavers—make sure you play the hooked quavers exactly on the third and sixth quaver beats (1,2,**3**,4,5,**6**).

Ellie's Jig

Practise the bowing patterns in this piece on open strings (see page 5–6). Watch out for the changes from C♯ to C♮—remember that accidentals only last for one bar.

RS

When Johnny Comes Marching Home

Count the tied notes carefully in bars 3–4 and 7–8: subdivide the dotted-crotchet beat and make sure the last note of the bar is played exactly on the 6th quaver.

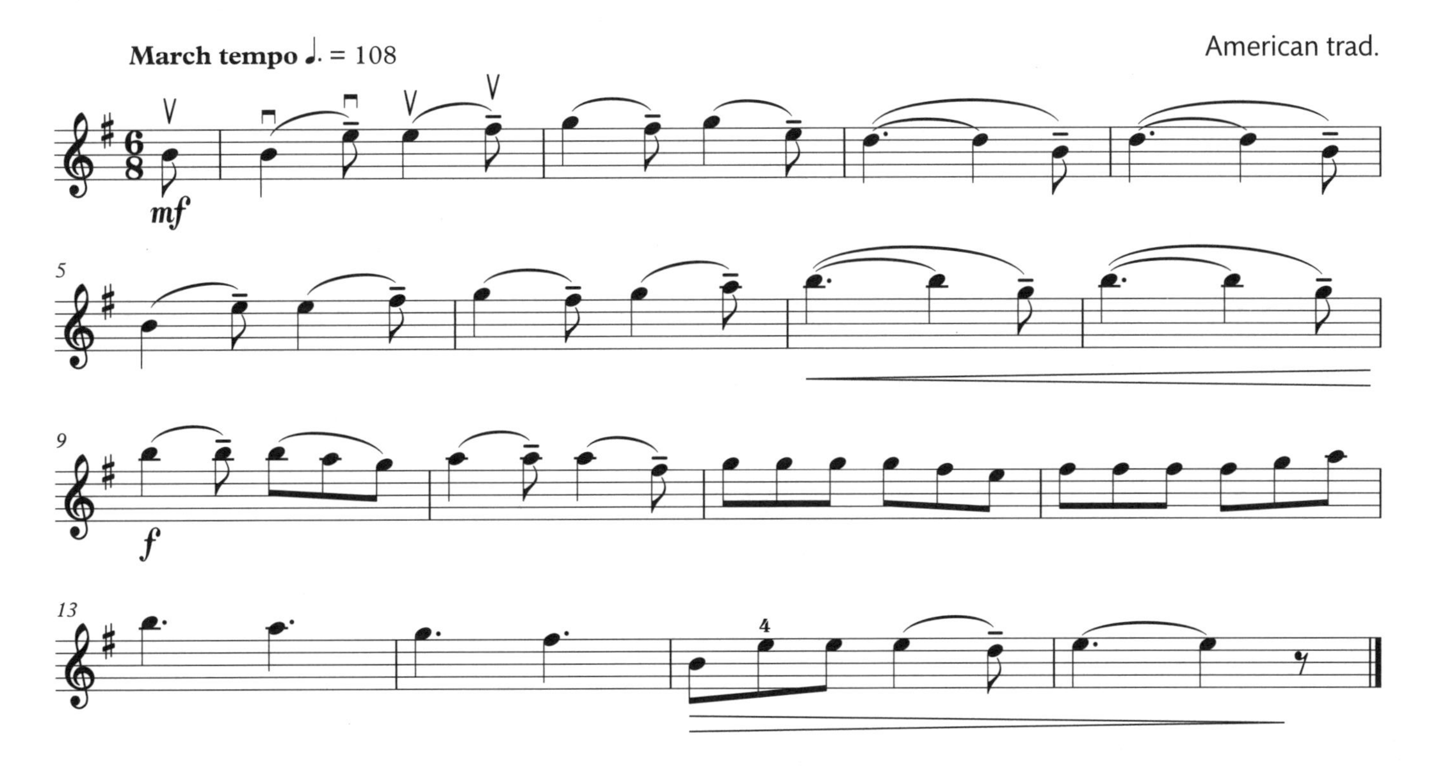

> **TECHNICAL TIP**
>
> When starting a piece or new phrase, particularly when starting on an up-bow, make sure the bow hair is in contact with the string fractionally before you start moving the bow—this contact can be gentle or strong depending on the dynamic and articulation of the first note. This is known as 'starting from the string' and helps to avoid bow crunches, or bow 'belly flops'!

TRY...

Try practising your scales in 6/8 time using hooked bow-strokes. The G major scale would start like this:

Staccato

Staccato notes are played shorter than written so that they're detached, or separated, from the next note. This is indicated with a dot above or below the note. Staccato is usually played on the string (i.e. the bow isn't lifted)—gaps between the notes are made by lightly stopping the bow on the string at the end of each stroke.

- The beginning of each note should be clearly articulated (without being accented)—say *ta-ta-ta-ta* to hear how this should sound (in contrast, non-staccato notes would sound like *taa-taa-taa-taa*). Make sure the bow hair catches the string cleanly at the beginning of each bow-stroke so that there is a crisp, clear start to each note.
- Note that the consonant sound is only at the **beginning** of each note, not the end, so the bow should 'bite' into the string only at the start of each bow-stroke.
- Staccato notes can be played shorter or longer, heavier or lighter, and with more or less articulation, depending on the tempo and your interpretation of the music.

Exercise 1: Playing short staccato bow-strokes

- Place your bow on the string at around the midpoint.
- Gently lean your 1st finger onto the bow stick so that the bow hair catches the string, then play a short down-bow stroke (approx. four inches). Make sure the beginning of the note is really clear, with no squeaks or crunches.
- Stop the bow lightly on the string at the end of the stroke, keeping your right-hand fingers relaxed.
- Catch the string again and play an up-bow stroke.
- Now play repeated staccato strokes. Start at ♩ = 100 and gradually increase the tempo, using less bow as you get faster. Try playing in different parts of the bow and at different dynamics.

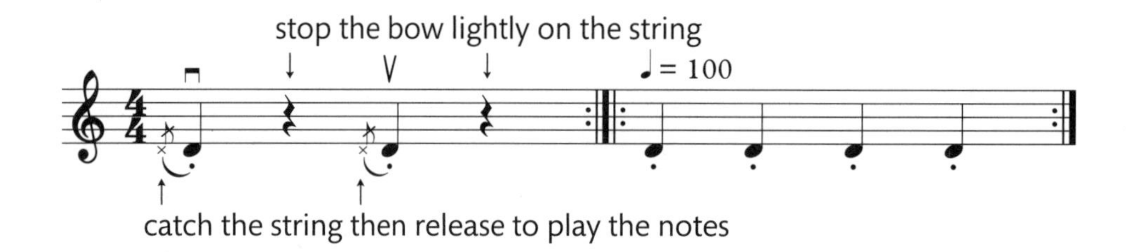

Exercise 2: Staccato scales

Try playing your scales with staccato bowing, starting at ♩ = 66 and gradually speeding up:

Exercise 3: Alternating between legato and staccato bow-strokes

Start at around the middle of the bow. Make as much contrast as you can between the short, light, detached staccato notes and the heavier, full-length tenuto notes.

TECHNICAL TIP

When playing music from the Classical period (e.g. Mozart and Haydn) and Baroque period (e.g. Bach and Vivaldi), a slightly staccato bow-stroke is often used to make the music sound light and dance-like. This articulation isn't usually marked in the score because it is assumed that musicians will interpret the music in this way, but in the pieces in this chapter it has been marked for guidance. Listen to some recordings of these pieces to hear how they are played.

Hooked bow-strokes with staccato dots

Until now hooked bow-strokes have been indicated with a slur and a line on the second, shorter note. You will also come across hooked bow-strokes marked with a slur and a dot. These are played in a very similar way, but when they are marked with a dot there is usually a bit more separation between the notes—this is achieved by making the first note shorter, or staccato. This may seem rather confusing, since the dot is written on the second note! Remember that the exact length of the notes is a musical decision; the notation should only be treated as a guide.

The Birdcatcher's Song from *The Magic Flute*   Track 3

Play this piece in the middle to upper half of the bow with short, light bow-strokes. Practise the slurred quavers with different rhythmic patterns to get the notes really even (see page 6). Play the dotted crotchets slightly staccato so that they are separated from the hooked quavers.

Wolfgang Amadeus Mozart (1756–91)

'Non più andrai' from *The Marriage of Figaro*

Make lots of contrast between the staccato and legato phrases in this piece. For the hooked staccato bowing in bars 1–5, 7–8, and 11–12 the dotted quavers should be played slightly shorter than written so that they are separated from the semiquavers.

Wolfgang Amadeus Mozart (1756–91)

Linked staccato up-bow strokes

Two or more consecutive staccato up-bow strokes between notes of the same length is known as linked staccato. In this technique, both notes are played equally short. Consecutive staccato down-bow strokes can also be played, but are less commonly used.

Linked staccato up-bow strokes on open strings 

- Play the phrase below with separate bows to start with, then with the marked bowing. Try to make the linked staccato quavers sound the same as the separate staccato quavers.
- Start at the middle of the bow at a slow tempo, using about eight inches of bow on each crotchet and half as much on each quaver, then gradually increase the tempo, making the bow-strokes shorter as the notes get faster.
- Stop the bow lightly on the string at the end of each up-bow stroke.
- Make sure the bow hair catches the string at the beginning of each bow-stroke so that all the notes start cleanly and crisply. The articulation in each bar should sound like *taa-ta-ta-taa-ta-ta*.

Trepak from *The Nutcracker*

Pyotr Ilyich Tchaikovsky (1840–93)

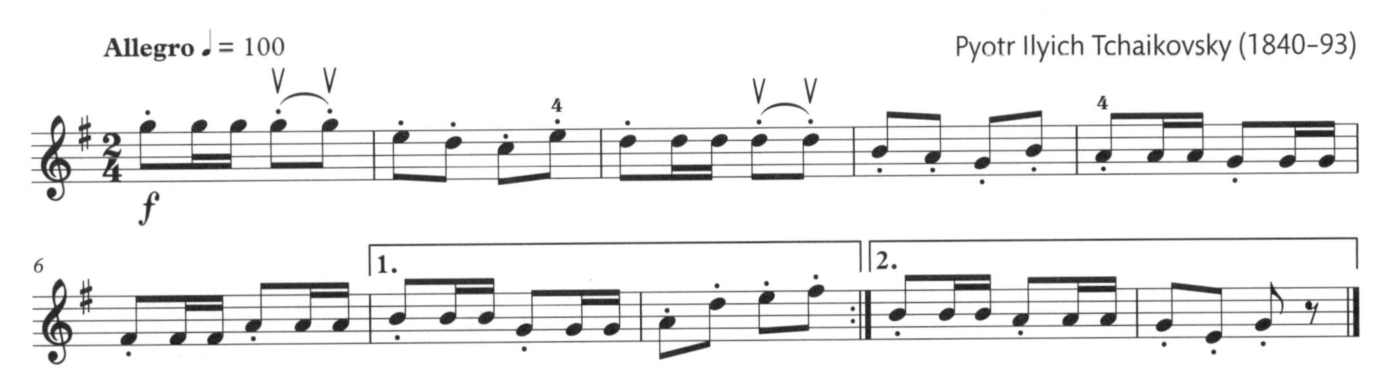

March from *Occasional Oratorio*

Practise the bowing on open strings to work on the staccato articulation and phrasing (see page 5–6).

George Frideric Handel (1685–1759)

3 HIGH 3RD FINGER

IN BOOK 1 you played with your 3rd finger in its low position. In this chapter you'll learn a new position for the 3rd finger, a semitone higher in pitch, which we'll call high 3rd finger.

High 3rd-finger notes

Finding the high 3rd-finger position

- Play a low 3rd finger on the D or A string, check its tuning with the open string below, and then step the finger a semitone up the fingerboard, away from the scroll.
- Move the finger up from the base knuckle, keeping your hand relaxed and taking care not to shift your thumb or the base of your 1st finger up the neck—widen the spaces between your 1st- and 2nd-, and 2nd- and 3rd-fingers to reach the note.
- Notice that the 3rd finger is now in a more extended, less square shape.

The 0--1--2--3-4 fingering pattern

Placing the 3rd finger in the high position gives rise to a new pattern of intervals between your fingers. Play this left-hand fingering pattern on all the strings and sing or say the note names for each string.

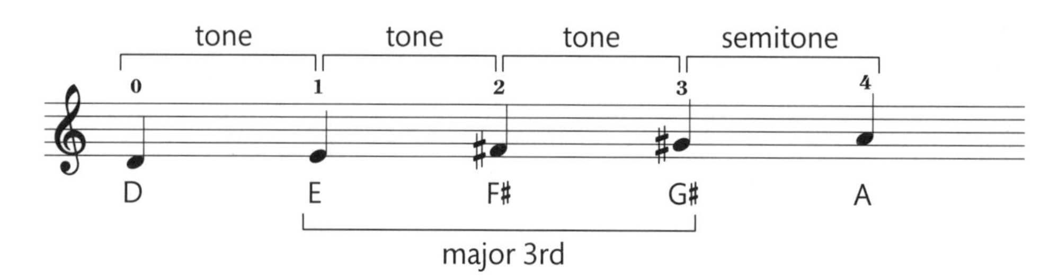

Look at the key signature!

Look out for high 3rd-finger notes when you see these key signatures. Find the keys on the circle of 5ths (page 100).

- **Two sharps** (F♯ and C♯): C♯ on the G string.
- **Three sharps** (F♯, C♯, and G♯): C♯ on the G string and G♯ on the D string.
- **Four sharps** (F♯, C♯, G♯, and D♯): C♯ on the G string, G♯ on the D string, and D♯ on the A string.
- **Five sharps** (F♯, C♯, G♯, D♯, and A♯): C♯ on the G string, G♯ on the D string, D♯ on the A string, and A♯ on the E string.

Exercise 1: Call and response

Work through the call and response exercise on the website, echoing back the notes you hear in the gaps.

Exercise 2: High 3rd-finger warm-up 

- Start by playing this exercise slowly using full, separate bow-strokes, listening carefully to your intonation. Check the tuning of 4th-finger As with the open string above. Then speed up, focusing on coordinating your right and left hands and playing rhythmically. Play with and without slurs.
- To start with, leave fingers down where marked, then repeat with only one finger on the string at a time. Keep unused fingers close to the strings, paying particular attention to your 4th finger.
- Repeat on the other strings using the same fingering pattern. Sing the note names for each string.

Exercise 3: Playing Mattachins (Sword Dance) by ear

- You learnt to play this melody in Book 1 (page 67). Play the first line again in this simplified version without slurs or dynamics (remembering to play the D with a low 3rd finger), and memorize it. There are demonstrations and backing tracks for this exercise on the website.

Peter Warlock (1894–1930)

- Now play it an octave lower, starting on 1st-finger A on the G string. The tune will sound the same, just in a lower register. Note that the C♯s are now played with a high 3rd finger instead of a high 2nd finger. Here are the first three bars to get you started:

- Now play the tune in the key of E major, starting on 1st-finger E on the D string. The fingering pattern is the same as in the previous version. Sing the note names.

- Finally, play it starting on 1st-finger B on the A string and on 1st-finger F# on the E string. Again, sing the note names for each string.

TRY...

Try playing 'Frère Jacques' starting on the 1st finger on the D or A string, or 'Mary had a little lamb' starting on a high 3rd finger on the G, D, or A string. Can you work out which key each version is in?

Kumbaya

This piece is in E major. Remember to play high 3rd-finger G# on the D string and listen carefully to the tuning of the semitone interval between your 3rd and 4th fingers. Count the tied notes carefully.

TRY...

Memorize 'Kumbaya', then play it in the key of A major, starting on 1st-finger A on the G string, then in the key of B major, starting on 1st-finger B on the A string. The fingering pattern is the same in each key. Sing the note names for each version.

Stowey

This piece is in B major—look out for high 3rd-finger D#s on the A string and G#s on the D string. Reach up for the 3rd-finger notes in plenty of time, keeping your hand relaxed.

Cielito Lindo

Track 9

There are high 3rd-finger notes on the E, A, and D strings in this piece. What are these notes called? Play the separate crotchets with light, slightly staccato bow-strokes.

Mexican trad.

Xiǎo Fàng Niú (The Young Shepherd Boy)

Track 10

This tune is an aria from a Peking opera, which is a form of Chinese theatre combining music, song, mime, dance, and acrobatics. Leave your 1st finger down where shown.

Chinese trad.

Playing with high and low 3rd finger

On each string the choice of high or low position for the 3rd finger depends on the key signature and any accidentals, and changing string will often mean a change of finger position. The next exercises and pieces include both high and low 3rd finger in the 0--1--2--3-4 and 0--1--2-3--4 fingering patterns. Carefully check which notes are affected by the key signature before you start each piece.

Exercise 1: Moving between 0--1--2--3-4 and 0--1--2-3--4 fingering patterns 

- Practise these exercises slowly, moving your 3rd finger between its high and low positions from the base knuckle while keeping your thumb and wrist relaxed.
- Check the tuning of low 3rd fingers with the open string below, and of 4th fingers with the open string above. Practise with and without fingers being left down.
- Repeat on the other strings using the same fingering pattern.

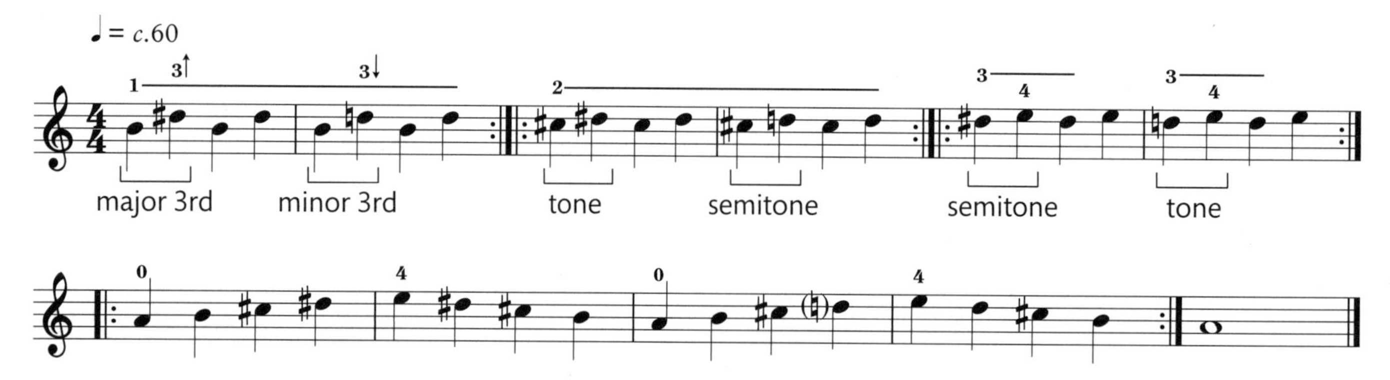

Exercise 2: Playing by ear

Play 'Happy Birthday' in the key of A major starting on 1st-finger E on the D string. You'll need to use high 3rd finger to play G♯ on the D string and low 3rd finger to play the D♮ on the A string near the end.

This piece is in E major. Use high 3rd finger to play D♯ on the A string and low 3rd finger to play A♮ on the E string. Watch out for the time signature changes—count two crotchet beats in the 2/4 bars.

This piece is in D major. Look out for high 3rd-finger C# on the G string and low 3rd fingers on the other strings. Slightly hold back the tenuto quavers in bar 13 to give them extra emphasis.

Playing with high and low 2nd and 3rd fingers

The next exercise and pieces use the 0--1--2--3-4 and 0--1-2--3--4 fingering patterns, which means both your 2nd and 3rd fingers moving between their high and low positions depending on which string you are playing on. Check the key signature and look out for accidentals before you start.

Exercise: Moving between 0--1--2--3-4 and 0--1-2--3--4 fingering patterns 

- Play this exercise slowly, keeping your left wrist and thumb relaxed.
- Repeat on the other strings using the same fingering.

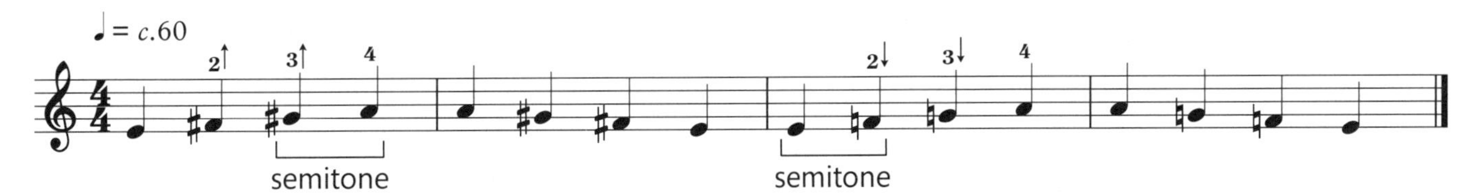

Greensleeves

Play this piece with plenty of bow. Start the first note in the lower half at around the balance point. When moving the bow from the D string to the E string during a quaver rest, lift it from the string (not too far–just 1-2 inches away) and carefully place it back down on the E string near the heel ready for the next note–take care to avoid any crunching sounds as the bow lands. Watch out for high and low 2nd and 3rd fingers.

English trad.

Why fum'th in fight

Track 14

This hymn melody was used by the British composer Ralph Vaughan Williams in his beautiful composition for string orchestra, Fantasia on a Theme by Thomas Tallis. *Listen to an orchestral recording of this piece. Clap the rhythm while counting a crotchet beat, and watch out for the tied notes in bars 16-17.*

Thomas Tallis (*c.*1505-85)

3rd-finger sliding semitones

To move between 3rd-finger notes a semitone apart on the same string, quickly slide (rather than lift) your finger up or down the string. The movement should come from the base knuckle of the finger. Practise this exercise with and without slurs. When playing with separate bows, the finger movement should happen at exactly the same time as you change bow so that there is no audible slide. When playing with slurs, make sure the finger movement doesn't disrupt the bow stroke.

Menuet from *Notebook for Nannerl*

Track 15

Leopold Mozart was a German composer and violinist, best known today as the father of Wolfgang Amadeus Mozart. He wrote this piece, originally for piano, for his daughter Nannerl. Look out for the sliding semitones in bars 1–2 and 3–4. Play the unmarked crotchets with light, slightly staccato bow-strokes at around the middle of the bow.

Leopold Mozart (1719–87)

Two-octave A major scale and arpeggio

- The **key signature** of A major is **three sharps**: **F♯**, **C♯**, and **G♯**.
- Use **high** 3rd fingers to play C♯ on the G string and G♯ on the D string.
- Use **low** 3rd fingers to play D on the A string and A on the E string. Make sure these notes don't sound sharp after playing the high 3rd fingers—check the tuning with the open string below.
- Say the note names out loud a couple of times while you play.
- Practise with and without the slurs.
- Use open strings to start with, then try using 4th fingers instead.

Long tonic

Even notes

Arpeggio

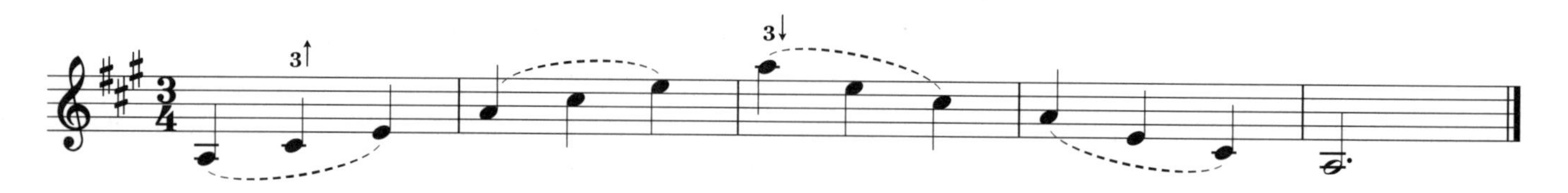

TRY...

Now try playing a one-octave E major scale and arpeggio, starting on 1st-finger E on the D string, and a one-octave B major scale and arpeggio, starting on 1st-finger B on the A string. The fingering pattern for both these scales is the same as for the lower octave of A major.

4 LOW 1ST FINGER

UP TO NOW you have played with your 1st finger in its 'high' position, a tone above the open string. In this chapter you'll learn a new position for the 1st finger, a semitone lower in pitch, which we'll call 'low' 1st finger.

Low 1st-finger notes

Remember that a flat sign ♭ lowers the pitch of a note by a semitone.

Finding the low 1st-finger position

Put your 1st finger down in the high position (a tone above the open string), then step it back towards the scroll to play a note a **semitone** above the open string, moving the finger from the base knuckle. Only the 1st finger should reach back—take care not to adjust your thumb or wrist position, otherwise you may have intonation problems with the other fingers.

The 0-1--2--3--4 fingering pattern

Play this new left-hand fingering pattern on all the strings. Sing the note names for each string.

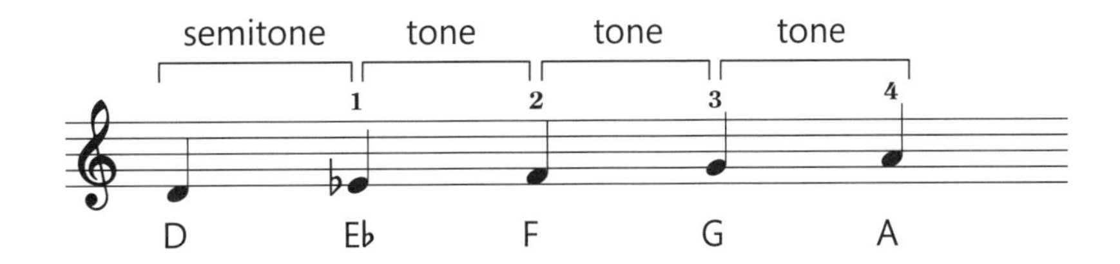

Look at the key signature!

Look out for low 1st-finger notes when you see these key signatures. Find the keys on the circle of 5ths (page 100).

- **No sharps or flats**: F♮ on the E string.
- **One flat** (B♭): F♮ on the E string and B♭ on the A string.
- **Two flats** (B♭ and E♭): F♮ on the E string, B♭ on the A string, and E♭ on the D string.
- **Three flats** (B♭, E♭, and A♭): F♮ on the E string, B♭ on the A string, E♭ on the D string, and A♭ on the G string.

Exercise 1: Low 1st-finger warm-up 

- Start by playing these phrases slowly, focusing on intonation and tone. Then speed up, focusing on coordinating your right and left hands and playing rhythmically. Play with and without slurs.
- To start with, leave fingers down where marked, then repeat with only one finger on the string at a time, keeping unused fingers close to the strings.
- Repeat on the other strings using the same fingering. Sing the note names for each string.

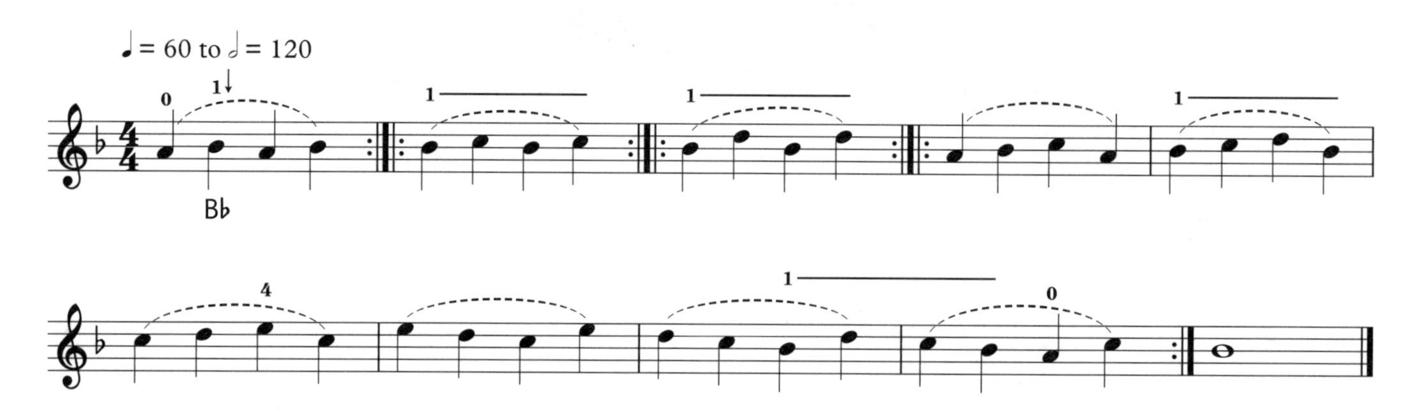

Exercise 2: Playing by ear

Play 'Mary had a little lamb' by ear, starting on 3rd-finger G♮ on the D string. What are the names of the 1st-finger notes you are playing?

Exercise 3: Call and response

Work through the call and response exercise on the website, echoing back the notes you hear in the gaps.

Arirang

This piece is in B♭ major. Reach back with your 1st finger in plenty of time to play B♭s on the A string and F♮s on the E string, keeping your wrist and thumb still and relaxed.

TECHNICAL TIP

Play this pentatonic scale slowly a few times to help with your intonation in 'Arirang'. Try making up your own pentatonic melody using these notes.

The Lawyer Outwitted

This piece is in a minor mode (a type of scale) called the ***Dorian mode****, which is often heard in folk music. The low 1st-finger notes are B♭ on the A string and E♭ on the D string.*

English trad.

TRY...

Try playing the C Dorian scale, which has the same key signature as B♭ major (two flats: B♭ and E♭—see page 37):

Trumpet Tune

This piece is in C major—remember that when there is no F♯ in the key signature you need to play low 1st-finger F♮ on the E string. Play bars 5–7 slowly a few times to get the intonation secure. Crotchets and dotted crotchets should be slightly staccato, as if played on a trumpet.

Henry Purcell (1659–95)

Sul tasto

Sul tasto means 'play over the fingerboard'. This creates a softer sound colour. The bow is usually placed about in line with the end of the fingerboard rather than over it, but try out different positions to find the sound that you think best suits the music. It's important to use light bow-strokes—if you press too hard the sound will become distorted. ***Normale*** means 'go back to playing in the usual manner'.

Arabic Dance

The low 1st-finger notes in this piece are A♭ on the G string and E♭ on the D string. Watch out for the change from B♮ to B♭ in bar 17. For an atmospheric effect try playing sul tasto *where marked.*

RS

Playing with low and high 1st finger

On each string the choice of low or high position for the 1st finger depends on the key signature and any accidentals, and changing string will often mean a change of finger position. The next exercise and pieces include low or high 1st fingers in the 0-1--2--3--4 and 0--1-2--3--4 fingering patterns. Carefully check which notes are affected by the key signature before you start each piece.

Exercise: Moving between 0-1--2--3--4 and 0--1-2--3--4 fingering patterns 

- Play these phrases slowly, keeping your left wrist and thumb still and relaxed as your 1st finger moves between its low and high positions.
- Repeat on the other strings using the same fingering pattern.

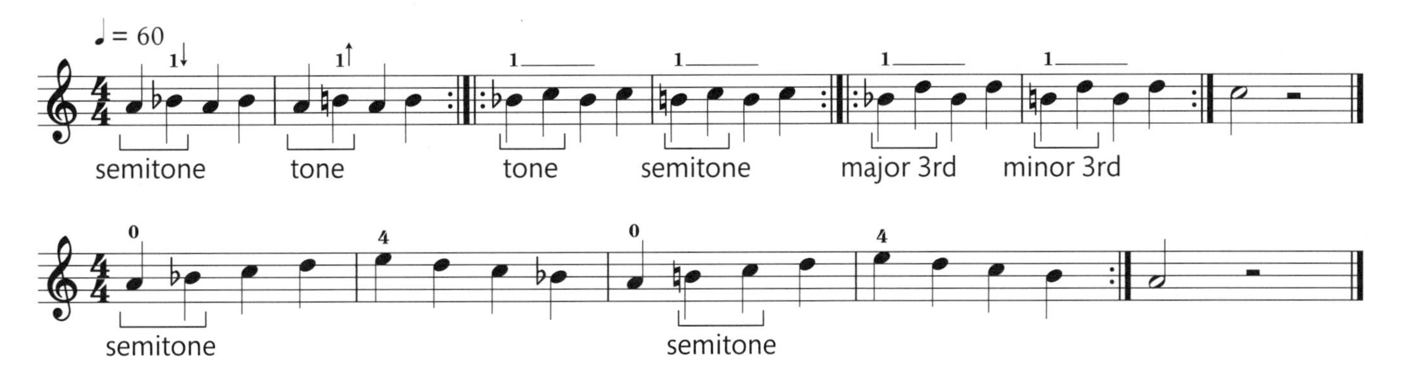

La Vera Sorrentina (The Fair Maid of Sorrento) 

This piece is in F major. Look out for low 1st-finger F♮s on the E string, low 1st-finger B♭s on the A string, and high 1st-finger E♮s on the D string. Use long, flowing bow-strokes for a legato, singing tone. Practise with a metronome to make sure the tied notes are well in time.

Italian trad.

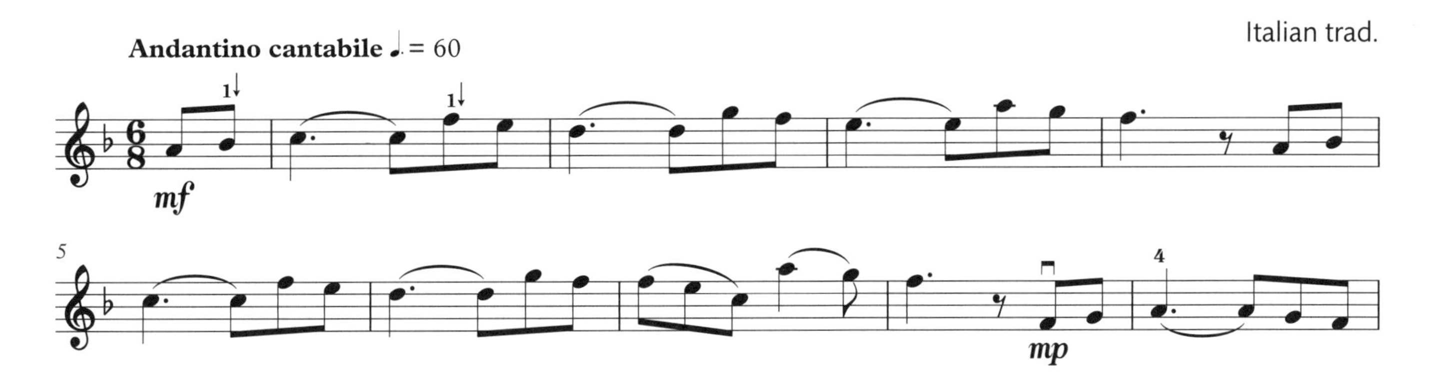

A Csitári Hegyek Alatt

Track 21

This piece is in A minor, which has no sharps or flats. There are low 1st-finger F♮s on the E string, high 1st-finger B♮s on the A string, and high 1st-finger E♮s at the D string. Use heavy, fast bow-strokes on the accented quavers; practise the bowing in the first four bars on open strings (see page 5–6).

1st-finger sliding semitones

Play this phrase with separate bows to start with, sliding your 1st finger (from the base knuckle) at exactly the same time as you change bow so that the slide isn't audible. Then add the slurs, making the sliding movement quick and smooth so that it doesn't disrupt the slur.

D.S. al Coda

D.S. al Coda means go back to the 𝄋 sign and then jump to the **coda** (which means 'tail' in Italian) when you reach the 𝄌 sign the second time through). Look out for this in the next piece.

Waltz from *The Sleeping Beauty*  

Watch out for sliding semitones between 1st-finger B♭ and B♮ and from 2nd-finger F♮ to F♯, and for the high 3rd-finger C♯ in bar 40.

Pyotr Ilyich Tchaikovsky (1840–93)

> **TECHNICAL TIP**
>
> When playing stopped notes a perfect 5th apart, the movement between the notes often sounds smoother if you place your finger in the space between the strings so that the outer edges of the finger touch both strings. If you have narrow fingers or are finding it difficult to get a clear sound it can help to lean the finger slightly towards the string you're playing on.

One-octave F major scale and arpeggio

- The **key signature** of F major contains one flat: B♭.
- Reach back with your 1st finger to play B♭ on the A string and F♮ on the E string.
- Say the note names out loud a couple of times while you play.

Long tonic

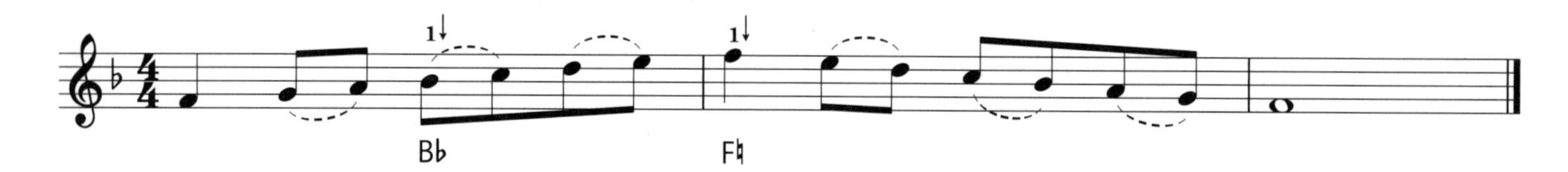

Even notes

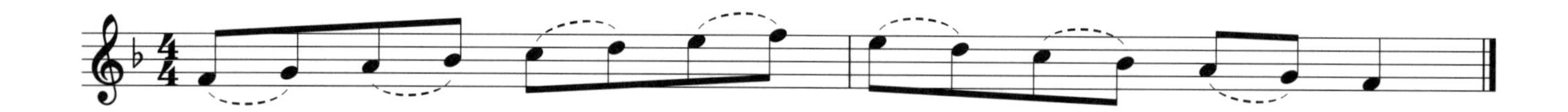

Arpeggio

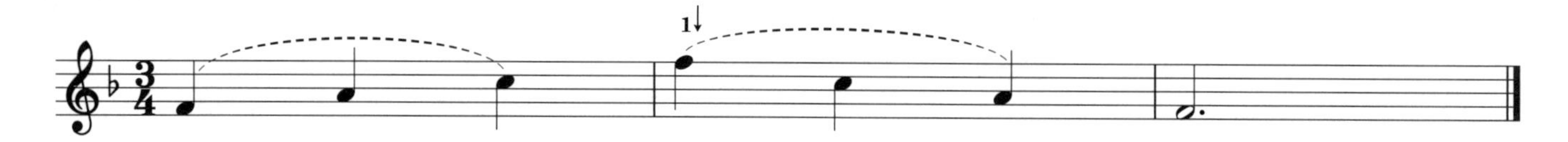

TRY...

Now try playing a one-octave B♭ major scale and arpeggio, starting on 2nd-finger B♭ on the G string (the key signature contains B♭ and E♭). Notice that the fingering pattern is the same as for the one-octave F major scale.

Extended C major scale (up to the dominant)

- The dominant is the fifth degree (or note) of a major scale.
- Remember that the **key signature** of C major contains **no sharps or flats**, so you need to use a low 1st finger to play F♮ on the E string.
- Keep your 1st finger nimble as it moves between its high and low positions.

5 LOW 4TH FINGER

UP TO NOW you have played with your 4th finger in its 'high' position a perfect 5th above the open string. In this chapter you'll learn a new position for the 4th finger, a semitone lower in pitch, which we'll call 'low' 4th finger.

Low 4th-finger notes 

Enharmonics

These low 4th-finger notes are the **enharmonic equivalents** of the high 3rd-finger notes you learnt in Chapter 3. Enharmonic notes are the same pitch but are spelt differently: **D♭ = C♯**; **A♭ = G♯**; **E♭ = D♯**; **B♭ = A♯**.

Finding the low 4th-finger position

- In its low position the 4th finger plays a note a semitone above the low 3rd finger and a semitone below the open string above.
- Play a low 3rd-finger note (C, G, D, or A), check its pitch, and then place your 4th finger close to the 3rd finger, listening carefully to the tuning.
- Your 4th finger should be quite upright and square in this position. Make sure both finger joints are curved.

The 0-1--2--3-4 fingering pattern

Play this new left-hand fingering pattern on all the strings. Note that all your fingers are now in their low positions. Sing the note names for all the strings.

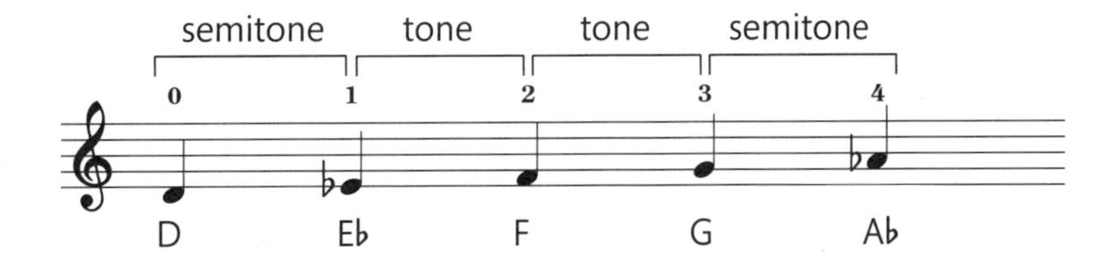

Look at the key signature!

Look out for low 4th-finger notes when you see these key signatures. Find the keys on the circle of 5ths (page 100).

- **One flat** (B♭): B♭ on the E string.
- **Two flats** (B♭ and E♭): B♭ on the E string and E♭ on the A string.
- **Three flats** (B♭, E♭, and A♭): B♭ on the E string, E♭ on the A string, and A♭ on the D string.
- **Four flats** (B♭, E♭, A♭, and D♭): B♭ on the E string, E♭ on the A string, A♭ on the D string, and D♭ on the G string.

TECHNICAL TIP

It's easy to misread a low 4th-finger E♭, A♭, or D♭ and play an open string by mistake. Always carefully check which notes are affected by the key signature before you start playing.

Exercise 1: Low 4th-finger warm-up 

- Start by playing these phrases slowly, focusing on intonation and tone. Then speed up, focusing on coordinating your right and left hands and playing rhythmically. Play with and without slurs.
- Keep unused fingers close to the strings—pay particular attention to your 4th finger.
- Repeat on the other strings using the same fingering. Sing the note names for each string.

Exercise 2: Call and response

Work through the call and response exercise on the website, echoing back the notes you hear in the gaps.

Exercise 3: Playing by ear

- Play 'Kumbaya' in E major as written on page 16, using 4th fingers where marked, and memorize it.
- Now play it again starting a semitone lower on low 1st-finger E♭. You're now playing in E♭ major, which has 3 flats: B♭, E♭, and A♭. Notice that the fingering and the intervals between your fingers are the same in both keys. Can you work out the names of the new notes you're playing?

Hungarian Dance No. 1

This piece is in the key of C minor, which is the relative minor of E♭ major (relative major and minor keys share the same key signature). Remember to play the A♭s on the D string with a low 4th finger. Use plenty of bow—lots of passion is needed for this tune! Feeling the pulse as one minim beat per bar helps give the music energy and momentum.

Johannes Brahms (1833–97)

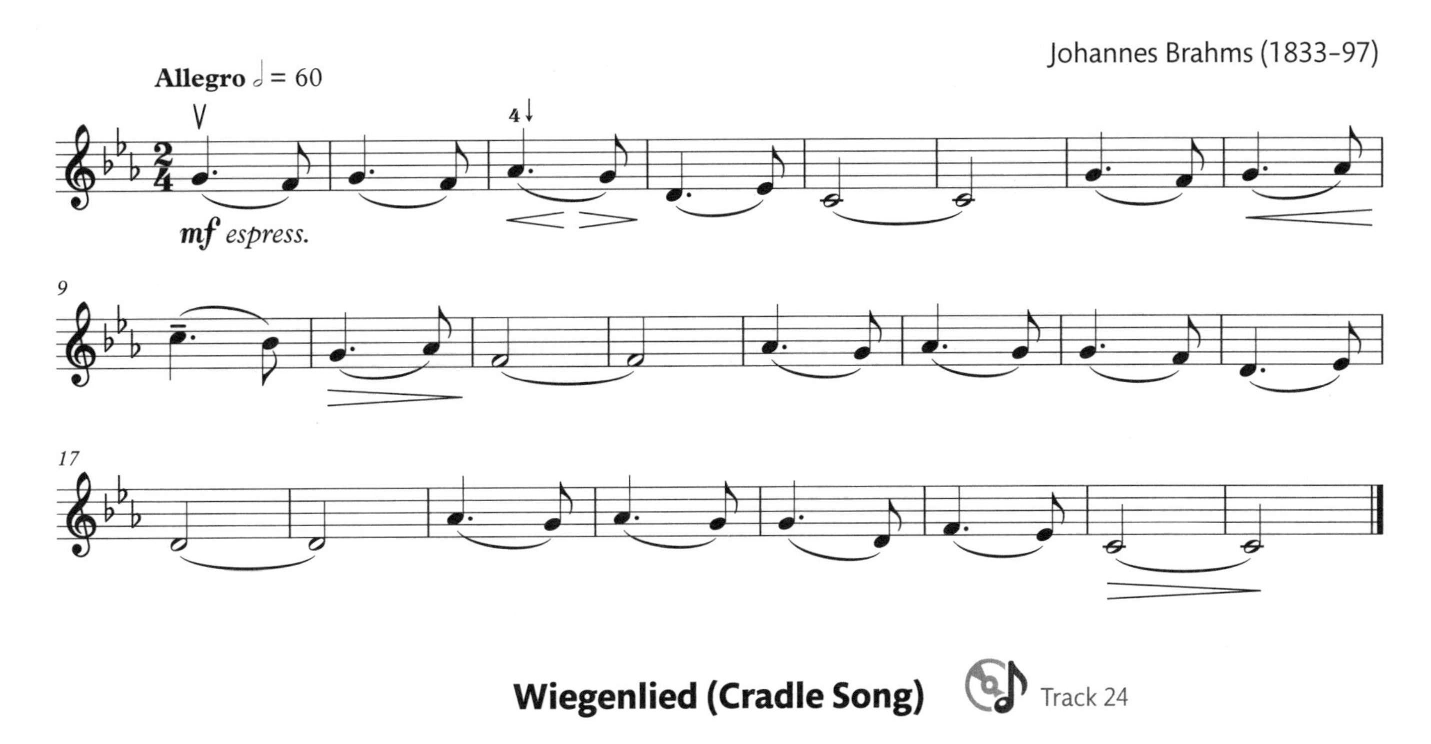

Wiegenlied (Cradle Song)

Track 24

*This famous lullaby should be played gently with flowing bow-strokes. Use a low 4th finger to play E♭s on the A string and B♭s on the E string. Try playing slightly sul tasto in the **p** bars for a really gentle sound. 'Zart bewegt' means 'with tender movement' in German. See the technical tip below for advice on intonation.*

Johannes Brahms (1833–97)

TECHNICAL TIP

This exercise will help you tune the B♭ octaves in bars 10–11 and 14–15 and the augmented 4th interval between 4th-finger E♭ and 3rd-finger A in bars 8–9 of 'Wiegenlied'. There's more about fingering these intervals on page 52.

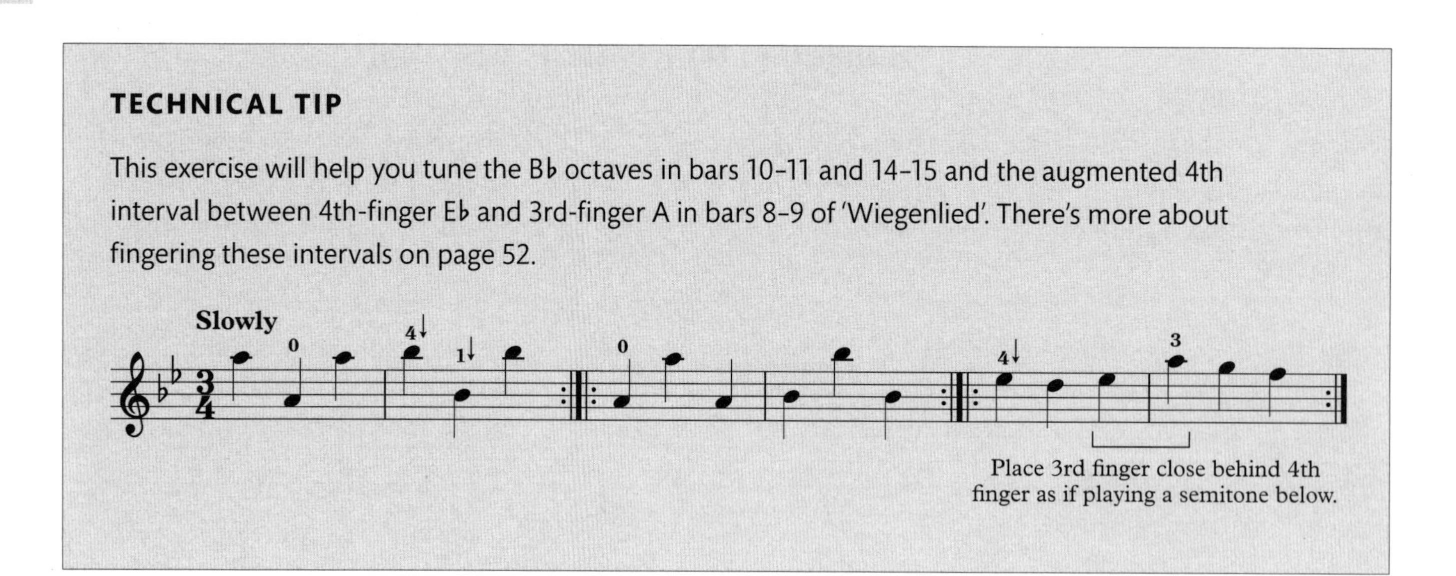

'Clair de lune' from *Suite bergamasque*

Track 25

This piece is in A♭ major. What are the names of the low 4th-finger notes on the A, D, and G strings? 'Con sord.' means 'with mute'—use your mute if you have one, as on the recording. Count the tied notes carefully—practise counting and clapping the rhythm of the melody along to the CD.

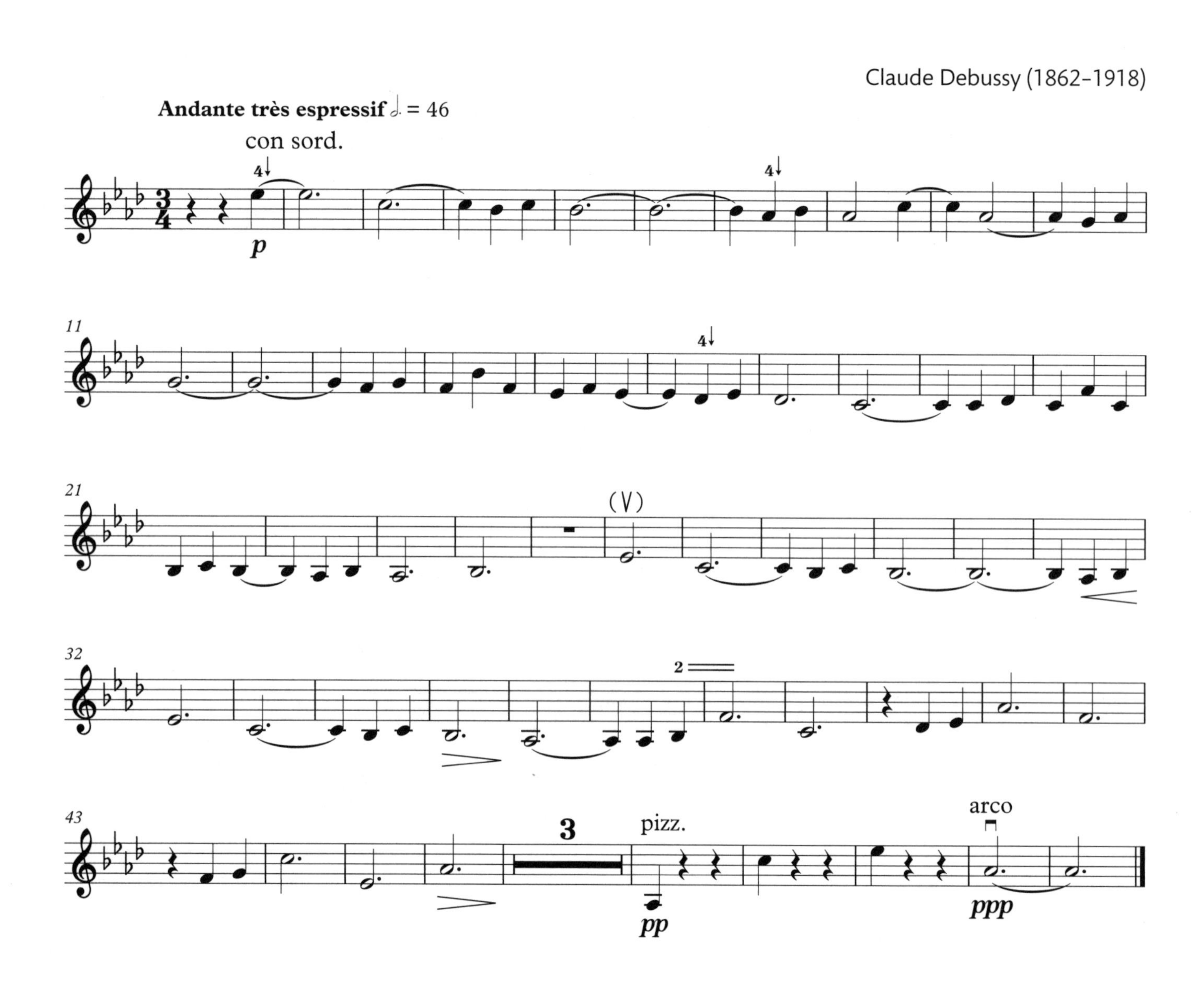

TECHNICAL TIP

To avoid running out of bow in a piece like 'Clair de lune', where the notes vary a lot in length, it's often necessary to 'save bow' on the long notes, i.e. use a slower and slightly heavier bow-stroke, and to 'move through the bow' on shorter notes, i.e. use a quicker, lighter bow-stroke. These changes in bow speed should not be noticeable to the listener. Try using a slightly faster, lighter bow-stroke on the up-bows during the first ten bars of 'Clair de lune' so that the long down-bows in bars 5–7 and 11–13 start near the heel. Save bow on the long notes, keeping the bow pressure and speed steady. Open-string practice with a metronome is very helpful for this kind of piece (see pages 5–6).

Playing with low and high 1st finger and low 4th finger

Look out for accidentals on 1st-finger notes in the next exercise and pieces. Your 1st finger will need to move between its low and high positions while your 4th finger remains in the low position.

Exercise: Moving between 0-1--2--3-4 and 0--1-2--3-4 fingering patterns 

Play this phrase slowly on all the strings. Move your 1st finger between its low and high positions from the base joint, keeping your left thumb and wrist still and relaxed.

London Ladies Track 26

This folk tune was first published in 1687, then later used by John Gay in The Beggar's Opera. *Play with small, neat bow-strokes at around the middle of the bow. Look out for the high 1st-finger F♯ in bar 11.*

English trad.

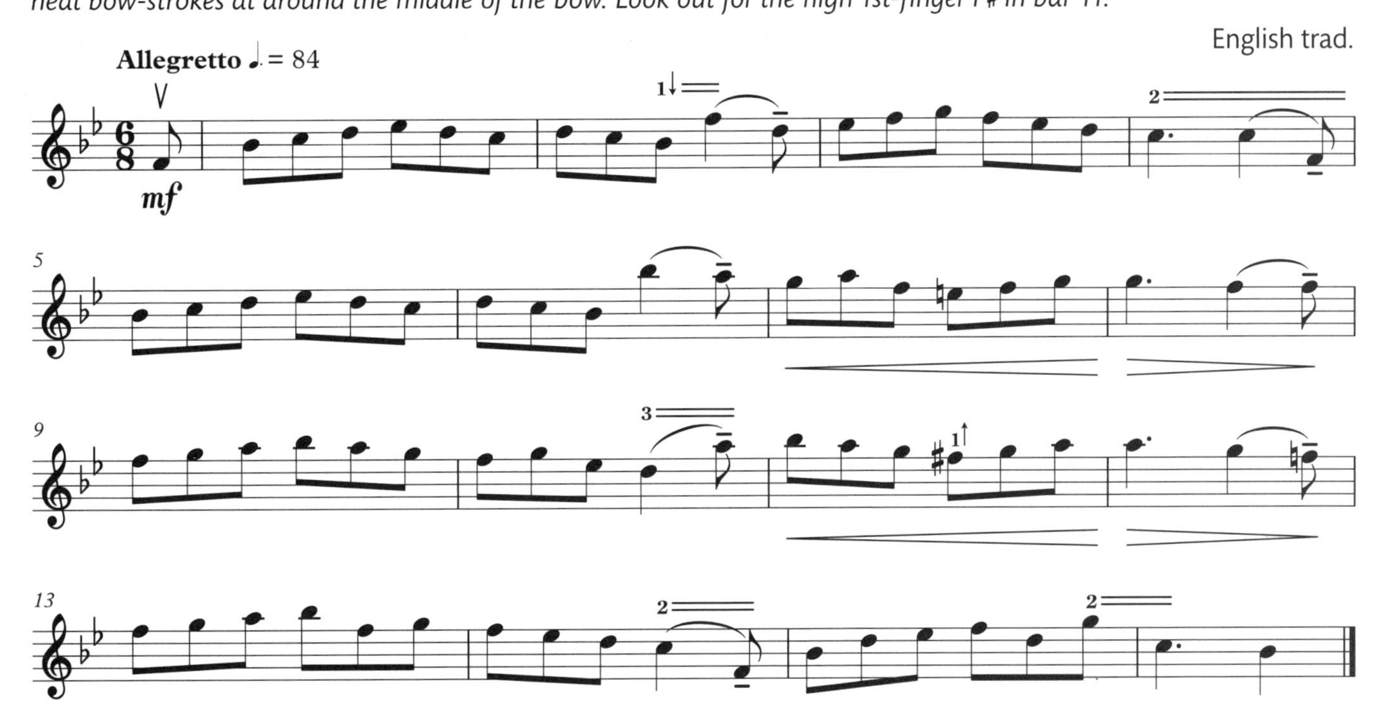

TECHNICAL TIP

Think of leading string crossings with your left hand so that the finger is always ready on the string fractionally before the bow starts moving. This will help you get a clear sound and is particularly important for the 4th finger, which can feel less agile than the other fingers.

Flow my tears

Track 27

This piece is by the English Renaissance composer John Dowland. Watch out for the changes between 1st-finger B and B♭ and remember that accidentals last for only one bar.

John Dowland (1563–1626)

Playing with low and high 4th fingers

On each string the choice of high or low position for the 4th finger depends on the key signature and any accidentals, and changing string will often mean a change of finger position. The next exercise and piece include high and low 4th fingers in the 0-1--2--3-4 and 0-1--2--3--4 fingering patterns. Carefully check which notes are affected by the key signature before you start each piece.

Exercise: Moving between 0-1--2--3-4 and 0-1--2--3--4 fingering patterns

- Play these phrases slowly, keeping your left thumb and wrist relaxed as your 4th finger moves between its high and low positions.
- Repeat starting on the D and G strings, using the same fingering.

Green Bushes

Track 28

Keep your 4th finger nimble as it moves between A♮ on the D string and E♭ on the A string.

Two-octave B♭ major scale and arpeggio

- The **key signature** of B♭ major contains **two flats**: **B♭** and **E♭**.
- Use a low 4th finger to play E♭ on the A string and B♭ on the E string.
- Play using an open D and an open A to start with, then try using a high 4th finger on these notes.
- Say the note names out loud a couple of times while you play.

TRY...

Now try playing one-octave E♭ major and A♭ major scales. The fingering pattern for these scales is the same as for the second octave of the B♭ major scale.

- E♭ major has a key signature of B♭, E♭, and A♭. Start on 1st-finger E♭ on the D string.
- A♭ major has a key signature of B♭, E♭, A♭, and D♭. Start on 1st-finger A♭ on the G string.

6 VIBRATO

IN THIS CHAPTER you will learn about **vibrato**, which is one of the most expressive techniques available to a violinist. Bear in mind that vibrato takes time and practice to develop, so don't rush it. Begin by working slowly on the basic vibrato movement—include exercises in your daily warm-up—and only move on to the 'Development of the vibrato movement' section when you are ready. In the meantime, continue working through the rest of the book—you aren't expected to achieve a perfect vibrato before starting Chapter 7! The longer you spend working on a slow, relaxed vibrato movement the better the final results will be. It is recommended that you also watch the vibrato tutorials on the *Violinworks* website.

What is vibrato?

- Vibrato is a left-hand technique consisting of a rapid rocking movement of a fingertip on the string to create a regular, pulsating change of pitch.
- Vibrato adds emotion and expression to the music, and warmth to the tone.
- Vibrato is characterized by the width and speed of the finger movement, ranging from slow and wide to fast and narrow. The kind of vibrato you choose to use for any given piece of music will depend on your personal interpretation of the music, and on the style of music you're playing.

Vibrato basics

- Vibrato is created by a movement of the arm or hand that 'rocks' or 'pulsates' the left-hand finger between the in-tune note and the same note slightly flattened. Vibrato shouldn't go sharper than the in-tune note because the ear perceives higher pitches more clearly, so your playing would sound out of tune.
- It's important to practise vibrato with only **one finger** down on the string at a time. Keep your other fingers relaxed and close to the strings.
- There are two main parts to the vibrato movement: a passive backward movement away from the in-tune note (towards the scroll) and an active forward movement that returns the finger to the in-tune note. As you vibrate, always focus on the **forward** movement.
- The vibrato movement can originate either from the wrist (known as hand vibrato) or from the elbow joint (known as arm vibrato). Both techniques are described here—try both and see which feels more natural for you. Some people use a combination of the two. However you do it, slow methodical practice, good posture, a secure and relaxed violin position, and a flexible and relaxed left hand are the keys to success.

Preparing for vibrato

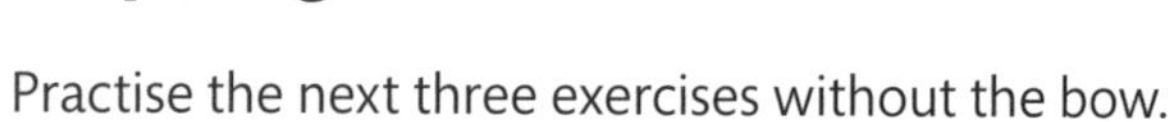

Practise the next three exercises without the bow.

Exercise 1: Check your posture and violin position

With your violin in position on your shoulder, check your posture, then drop your arms down by your side and relax your shoulders. Breathe deeply in and out. If your violin feels as though it might slip off your shoulder, adjust its position and repeat the exercise until it feels totally secure and comfortable. This is important because vibrato is difficult to do if you're lifting your shoulder to hold the instrument in place.

Exercise 2: Flexibility of the top joints of the fingers 

The top joint of the finger plays an important role in vibrato: it needs to be flexible so that the finger pad can roll up and down the string without sliding. This exercise will help you get used to the feeling of moving this joint.

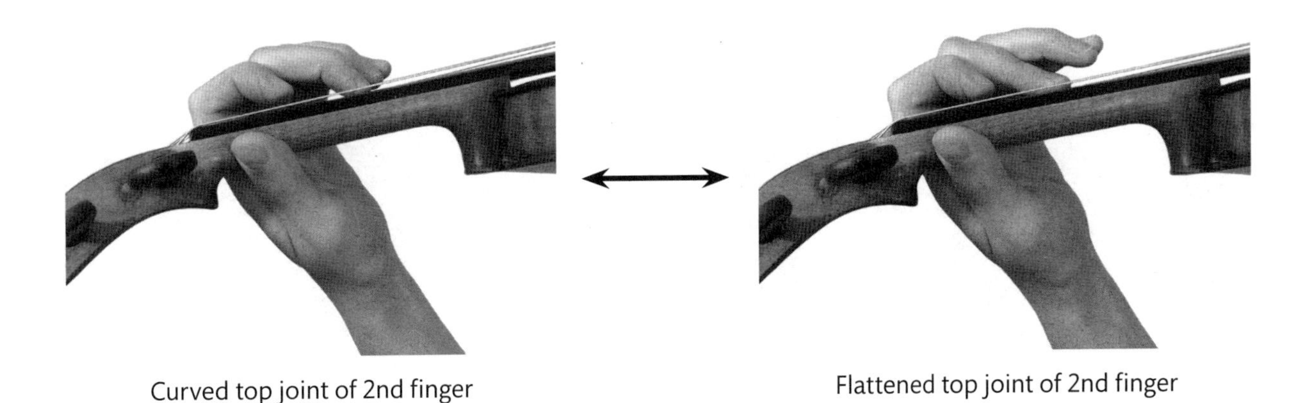

Curved top joint of 2nd finger

Flattened top joint of 2nd finger

- Place your 2nd finger on the A string in the C♯ position, making sure the joints are curved.
- Gently flatten (collapse) the top joint of the finger (the one nearest the nail) without moving any other part of the finger or the hand, then return it to its usual curved shape. Repeat several times in a continuous, regular movement.
- Notice that the finger pad rolls back slightly as the joint flattens.
- Repeat with your other fingers, placing them one at a time on the A string, then repeat on the other strings.

Exercise 3: The basic vibrato movement 

You may find it helpful to rest the scroll of the violin gently against a wall when you first try this exercise, to keep the violin stable, but make sure the violin is positioned correctly on your shoulder. Regularly stop and check that your left shoulder is relaxed by dropping your arm down by your side as described above.

- Place your 2nd finger lightly in the C♯ position on the A string and check your left-hand position: your hand should be relaxed, the finger joints curved, the side of your thumb (above the top joint) should rest against the neck, and the crease at the base of your 1st finger should rest against the E-string side of the fingerboard. No other part of your hand should touch the neck. Your wrist should be loose and in line with your hand and forearm, and your elbow should hang freely under the violin.
- Now slide your whole hand as a unit (including your thumb) up and down the neck of the violin so that your 2nd finger pad slides up and down the string. Do this either by moving your hand from the wrist in a waving motion (for hand vibrato), or by moving your forearm from the elbow (for arm vibrato). Keep your 2nd finger curved (don't move it independently of the hand), and keep unused fingers over the strings.
- Can you feel the crease at the base of your 1st finger sliding along the E-string side of the fingerboard?
- Gradually reduce the width of the sliding movement to about two inches. Then keep your thumb still, resting it about half-way up the neck, while your hand and finger continue to slide. Focus on moving the base of your 1st finger between the following positions: opposite the thumb (in the normal playing position) and about two inches back towards the scroll. The joint at the base of the thumb is now acting as a hinge, allowing the hand to move. This flexibility of the thumb base joint is very important in vibrato.

- Further reduce the sliding movement of your hand to a width of about one inch, then leave your finger pad in one spot on the string (as if playing a note) while continuing to move your hand: the crease at the base of your 1st finger should continue to slide up and down the E-string side of the fingerboard while your thumb and finger pad remain in place. Allow the top joint of the finger to flatten as your hand moves back towards the scroll, then return it to its usual curved shape as your hand moves forward again into its normal playing position—this creates a 'rolling' movement of the finger pad on the string. This is the basic vibrato movement.
- Repeat this basic vibrato movement many times until it begins to feel natural.
- Repeat on the other strings and with the 3rd, then 1st, then 4th finger.

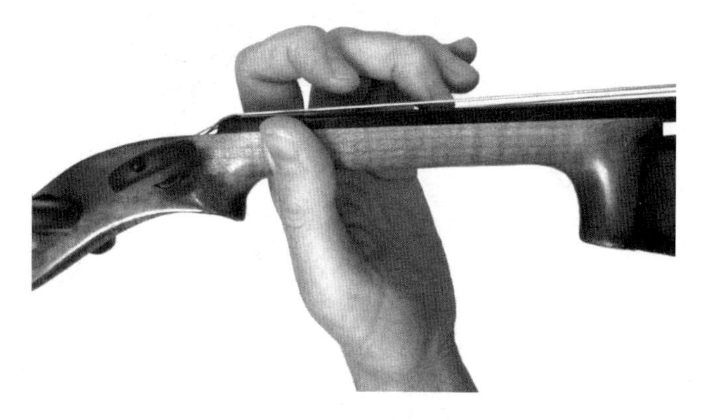

'Forward' vibrato position for 2nd finger:
'Normal' playing position with the 2nd finger in a curved, upright position, and the base of the 1st finger opposite the thumb.

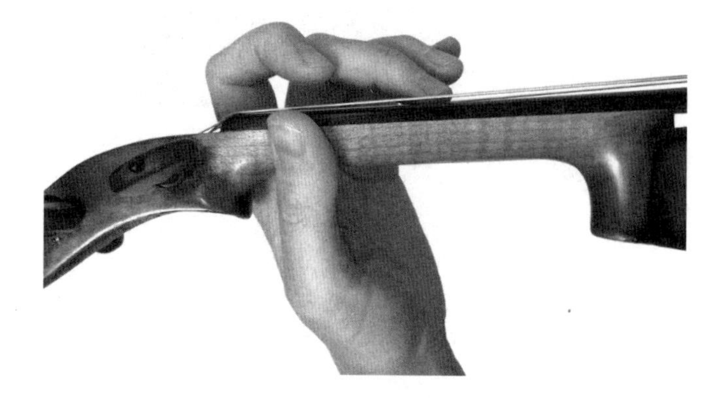

'Back' vibrato position for 2nd finger:
The base of the 1st finger slides back towards the scroll, pulling the 2nd-finger top joint flat and rolling the finger back. Notice that the thumb position hasn't changed and that the hand, wrist, and forearm are still in line.

In the next exercise you'll practise the basic vibrato movement very slowly with the bow.

Exercise: Call the emergency services!

- Start on the in-tune note, allow your hand to drop back and the top joint of your finger to flatten so that the note goes flat, and then move your hand forward again to return to the in-tune note and the finger's normal, curved position. It's important to focus on this forward movement when playing vibrato.
- Play two vibrato pulses per bow-stroke with an even rhythm, as shown below. You'll sound a bit like an ambulance siren. Repeat many times until it feels natural.
- Repeat the steps described above, this time in a dotted rhythmic pattern, making the flattened note shorter than the in-tune note.
- Repeat with the 3rd, then 1st, then 4th finger, and on the other strings.

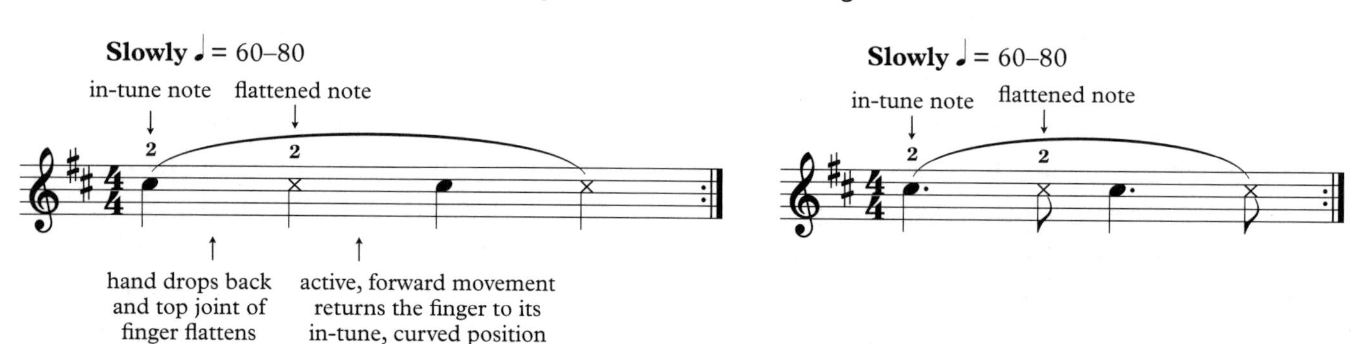

TECHNICAL TIPS

- When playing 1st-finger vibrato take extra care not to grip the violin neck between your thumb and 1st finger.
- When playing 4th-finger vibrato make sure the middle joint stays curved, and don't press too hard.
- Listen very carefully to your tuning. The finger should just rock to and fro on the string; it shouldn't slide along the string, otherwise the note will go out of tune.
- Your violin shouldn't shake when you play with vibrato—if it does then you are probably gripping the neck too tightly. Stay relaxed!

Development of the vibrato movement 

Don't try this section until you can do the last two exercises effortlessly—it's easy to get into bad habits if you try to speed up the vibrato movement too soon.

Exercise 1: Speeding up your vibrato

- Continue practising your vibrato with a dotted rhythm as described in the exercise above, but make the hand and finger movement smaller so that you are only partially flattening the top joint of the finger. Set your metronome to 𝅗𝅥 = 60 and play two vibrato pulses per beat, as shown below.
- Gradually make the vibrato movement quicker, speeding up your metronome a little at a time. Keep your bow speed constant: as you increase the tempo, play more vibrato pulses in each bow stroke until you are playing eight pulses per bow. If you feel your hand getting tense, slow the vibrato down again.

Gradually speeding up 𝅗𝅥 = 60–120

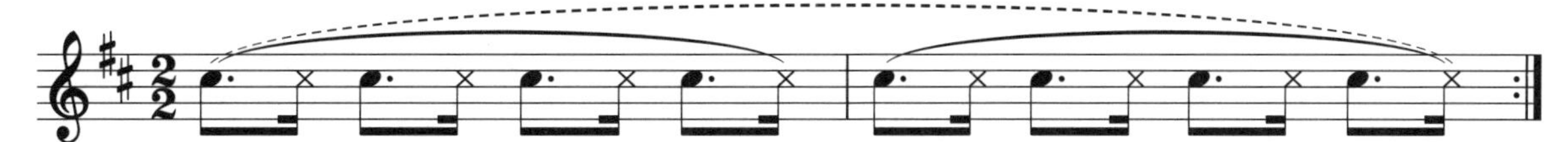

Exercise 2: Trying out your vibrato

- When the previous exercise begins to feel easy, try adding a little vibrato to the longer notes in your pieces, in particular in more romantic or lyrical styles of music.
- Include scales with vibrato in your practice routine. Play them with even notes and slow, full bow-strokes. Don't always practise your scales with vibrato, though, as this can make it harder to focus on intonation.

Exercise 3: Varying the speed and width of your vibrato

- As you gain confidence, try out different speeds and widths of vibrato: slower and wider, faster and narrower.
- Experiment with changing the part of your fingertip that is in contact with the string: a flatter finger for wider vibrato; a more upright finger for narrower vibrato.

7 NEW BOWING TECHNIQUES PART 2

Hooked bow-strokes in syncopated rhythms

Hooked bow-strokes are often used when playing syncopated rhythms.

- Clap these syncopated rhythms along to your metronome, then play them on an open string using the marked bowing, starting at around the middle of the bow.
- Use heavier, faster bow-strokes on the accented quavers and return the bow to its starting point on the repeat of each phrase.

Linstead Market

Track 29

Practise the bowing in the first four bars on open strings with a metronome to make sure it's really rhythmic.

Roda de Choro

Track 30

Choro is a style of Brazilian folk music, characterized by syncopated rhythms and upbeat melodies. Look out for hooked bow-strokes, retakes, sliding semitones, and the top E harmonic at the end.

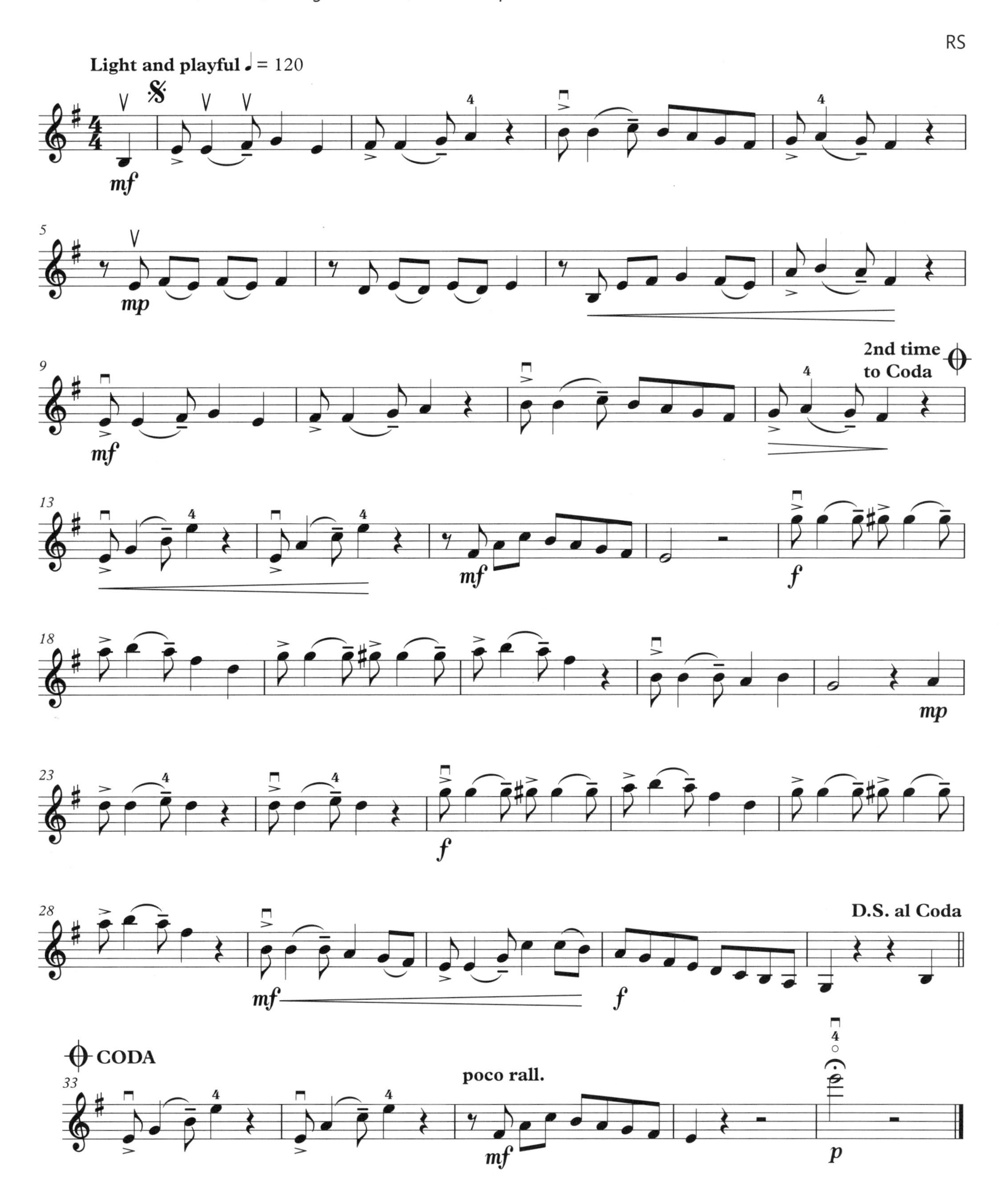

Playing three linked staccato up-bow strokes

Several consecutive staccato up-bow strokes are often played to move the bow towards the heel ready for a strong downbeat or long down-bow stroke. As with pairs of linked staccato up-bow strokes, the bow hair should catch the string cleanly at the beginning of each note, and the bow should be stopped lightly on the string at the end of each note.

- Play the following phrase, starting in the upper half of the bow. Use about the same amount of bow on each up-bow crotchet, and travel through the bow so that you reach the heel for the beginning of the next bar, ready to play the dotted minim. Keep your right-hand fingers relaxed and curved as you approach the heel.
- Play the dotted minim with a long bow-stroke so that the bow returns to its starting point.
- Keep the strokes light—the articulation over the two bars should be *ta-ta-ta-taaa*.

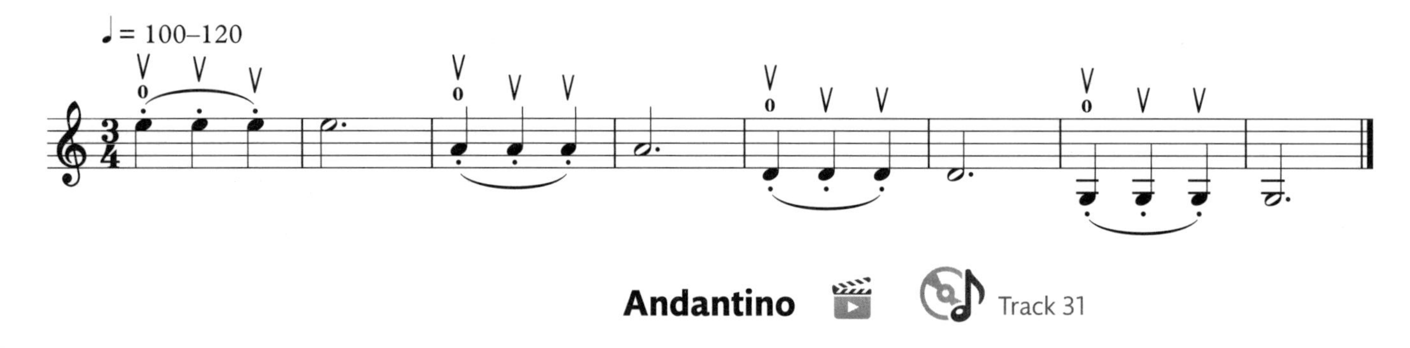

Andantino

Track 31

Start this piece at around the balance point of the bow and use plenty of bow on the down-bow minims. When playing the linked staccato up-bow crotchets, travel through the bow so that you return to the balance point by the beginning of the next bar.

Martelé bow-strokes

Martelé literally means 'hammered'. This technique is characterized by an accented, almost percussive start to the note and is most often used when playing accented notes at a ***f*** or ***ff*** dynamic.

- **Short** *martelé* bow-strokes are basically accented staccato strokes: short, separated notes with a strong 'bite' at the beginning of each stroke.
- **Long** *martelé* bow-strokes also have a strong attack but there is usually less separation between them: the initial attack is made with a strong 'bite' and a fast bow speed, immediately followed by a slower, sustained bow movement. Full, or nearly full, bow-strokes are often used.

Exercise: Playing short and long *martelé* bow-strokes 

- Start by practising the short *martelé* bow stroke, then try the long *martelé* bow stroke.
- Rest your bow on the string at around the balance point, ready to play a down-bow.
- 'Bite' the bow into the string by leaning your arm onto the side of your index finger. Feel the friction between the bow and the string by silently pulling the string to the side—can you feel the hair gripping the string?
- Release the bow with a fast, heavy stroke, immediately reducing the speed and pressure of the bow on the string after the initial attack. The aim is to get a clear 'bell-tone' or 'ka' sound at the beginning of the stroke. Use around 6-8 inches of bow for the short *martelé* strokes (using less bow as the tempo increases) and lots of bow for the long *martelé* strokes.
- At the end of the stroke stop the bow silently on the string, let your hand relax, and then repeat on an up-bow. You'll need a bit more arm weight to achieve the same effect higher up the bow.
- Gradually make the gaps between the notes shorter until you are playing continuous notes, as shown.
- If your sound is scratchy, try using a bit less pressure on the string. Also check your contact point—make sure you're not too close to the fingerboard or bridge.

Short *martelé* strokes

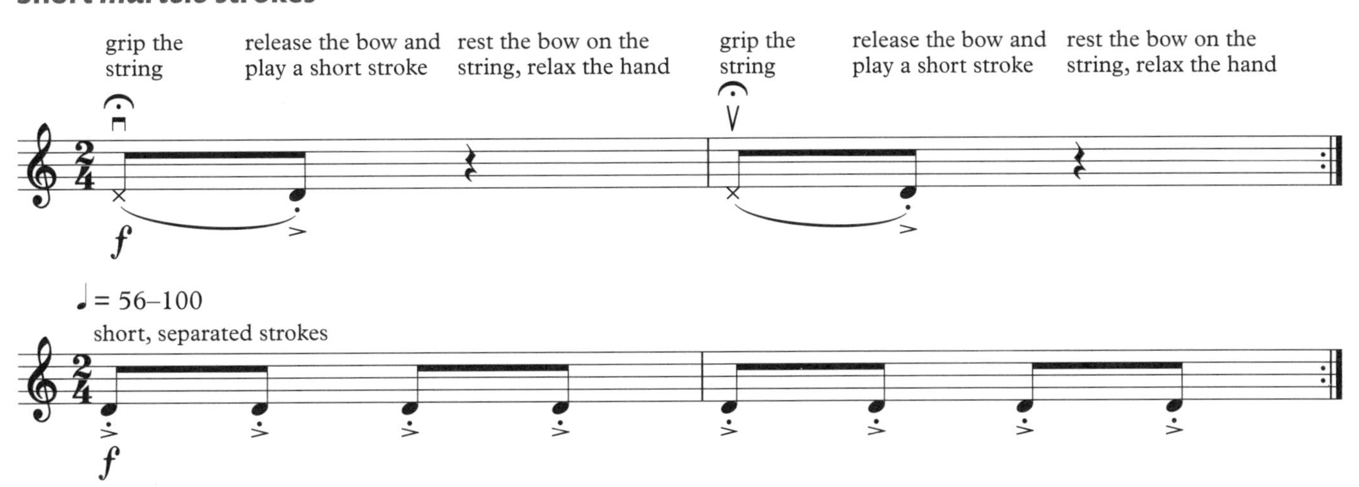

Long *martelé* strokes

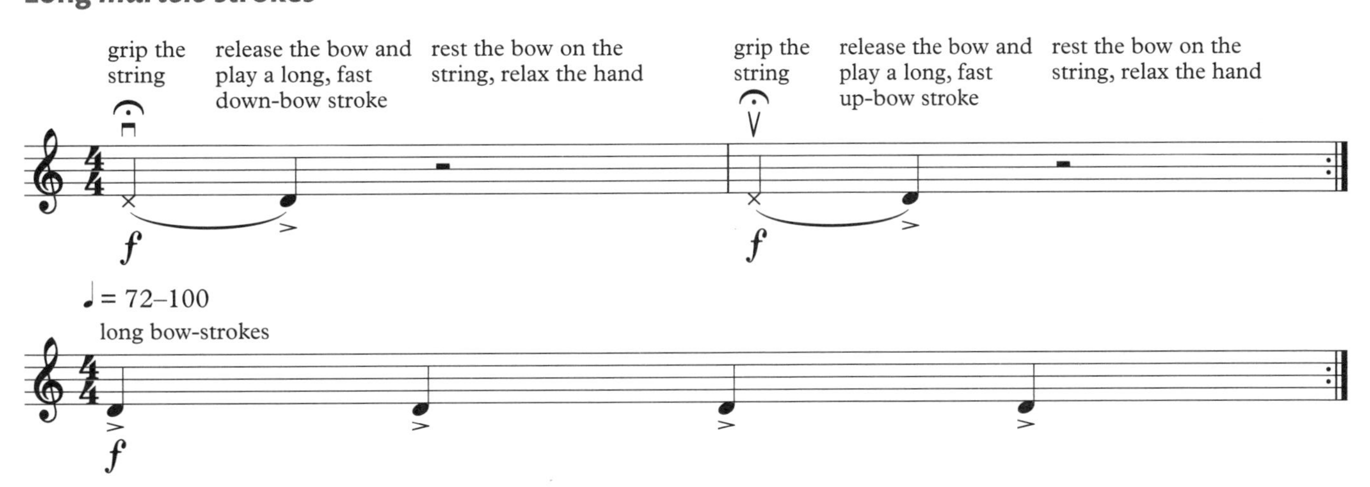

Sforzando

Sforzando, or ***sf***, means play the note with a sudden, strong emphasis. It is like an accent, but usually has a greater element of surprise, or contrast. Use a *martelé* bow-stroke to play *sforzando* notes.

Theme from *Marche Militaire No.1*

Track 32

*In the **f** sections play the accented, staccato quavers with short* martelé *bow-strokes and the **sf** minim and accented crotchets with long* martelé *bow-strokes.*

Franz Schubert (1797–1828)

Crossing more than one string

It's often necessary to move the bow between the G string and the A string or E string, or between the D string and the E string, without a rest between the notes. This can be done without lifting the bow off the string: make a quick string-crossing movement from the shoulder so that the momentum of your arm moves the bow over the middle string(s) without it sounding.

- Move your whole arm as a unit from the shoulder so that your right elbow stays level with your bowing hand as you cross the strings.
- To start with, play the notes staccato or *martelé* with a moment of silence at the end of each note, then try playing them more legato with less of a gap.
- Play with short bow-strokes in the lower half, middle, and upper half, and with longer bow-strokes.
- Be sure to catch the string with the bow hair before moving the bow. This is particularly important on the lower strings, which are likely to squeak if there isn't enough arm weight on the bow.

Martelé and String-Crossing Study

Use full martelé *bow-strokes for the crotchets in the* ***f*** *sections and slightly less bow in the* ***mf*** *sections. When it's sounding really good at the slower tempo, speed it up, but try to use the same amount of bow on each crotchet so that you're playing with fast bow-strokes. The quavers are not* martelé*, and can be played with quite short bow-strokes. Move your whole arm as a unit on the string crossings, always making sure that your left hand is ready on the string and your right elbow is level with your bowing hand before you play the note. Watch out for the low 1st-finger A♯s in bars 2, 6, 18, and 22.*

8 AUGMENTED 2NDS AND DOMINANT 7THS

Augmented 2nds

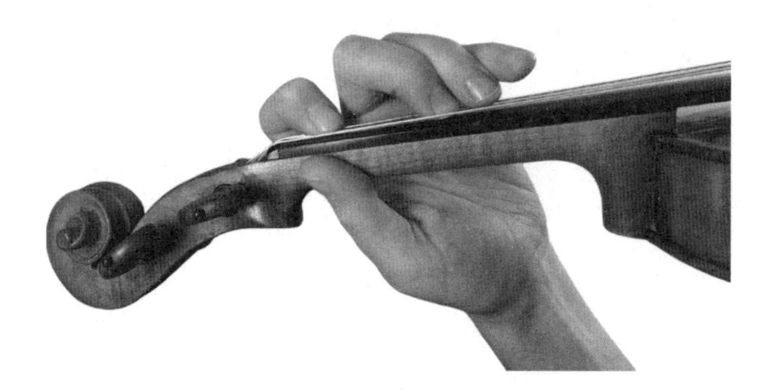

In this chapter you'll learn to play an augmented 2nd between your 1st and 2nd fingers. An augmented 2nd is an interval of three semitones, or a tone and a half (see page 5). 'Augmented' simply means bigger, and you will experience this as a bigger than usual gap between two fingers.

The 0-1---2-3--4 finger pattern 

- Play this left-hand fingering pattern on all the strings.

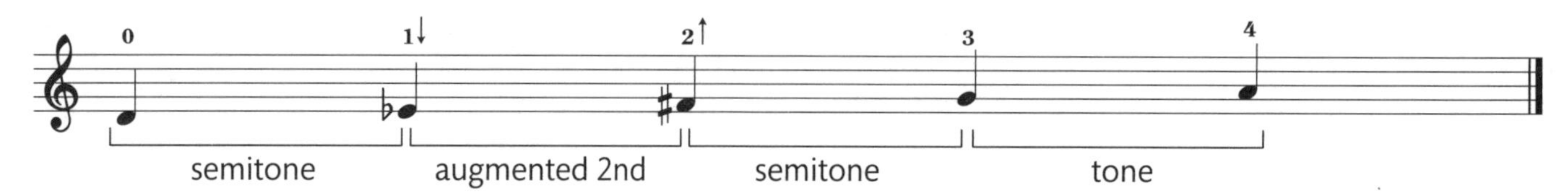

- Reach back from the base knuckle to play the low 1st finger and forward from the base knuckle to play the high 2nd finger, keeping your left thumb and wrist relaxed.
- Sing the note names on each string.

Exercise: Augmented 2nd warm-up

- Play this exercise on all the strings, starting slowly and then increasing the tempo.
- Play with separate bows at first, then try slurring two, then four, notes to a bow, joining the notes together as smoothly as you can.

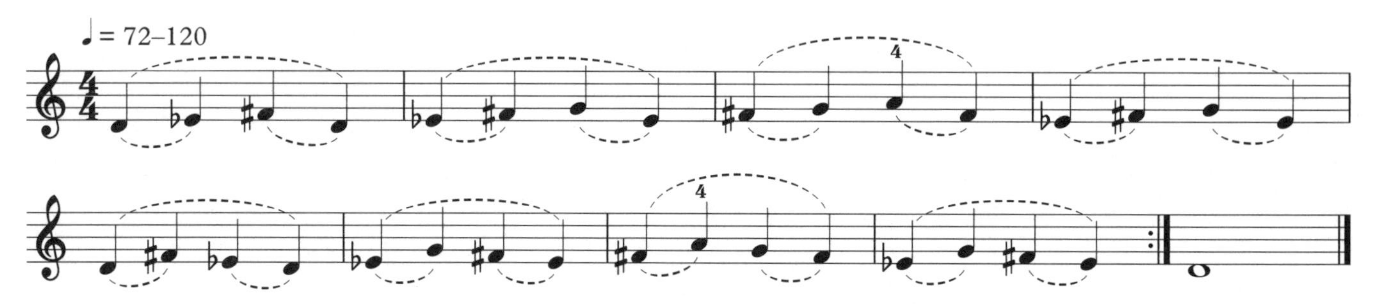

Guanabara Bay

Track 33

This piece is in the style of a Brazilian bossa nova. Look out for the augmented 2nd intervals between F♯ and E♭ in bars 2 and 18. Sing the words along to the recording to help with the rhythm.

Kaveri Kriti

Track 34

'Kaveri Kriti' is based on a South Indian Carnatic song form called a kriti. *A* kriti *is usually made up of three sections:* pallavi *(like a refrain in Western music),* anupallavi *(first verse), and* charana *(second and longest verse, often followed by an improvisation). Look out for the augmented 2nd intervals between C♯ and B♭.*

TRY...

Indian music uses **ragas** instead of scales; the raga specifies the notes to be used in a piece as well as other details such as ornamentation, mood, or even the time of day when it should be played. 'Kaveri Kriti' uses the Sarasangi raga, which has an augmented 2nd between the sixth and seventh notes; it's like a D major scale but with a B♭. Try playing it:

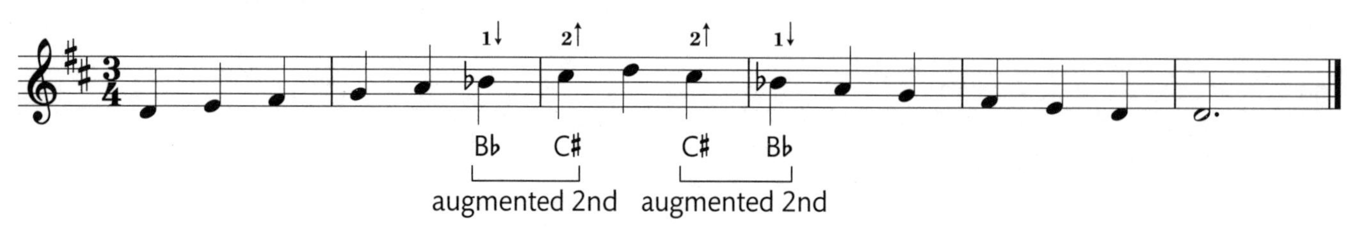

Indian musicians often perform long improvisations in their performances; they improvise using the notes of the raga that the piece is based on. Have a go at improvising your own melody using the notes of the Sarasangi raga. Pick three notes from the raga and play them with a simple 3/4 rhythm (e.g. two crotchets and two quavers). As you get more confident, try adding more notes from the raga and changing the rhythm. There is a backing track on the website.

Dominant 7ths

If you've ever played the guitar you've probably already come across dominant 7th chords, for example G7 or D7. The function of the dominant 7th chord in music is to resolve to the tonic (home) chord. This chord progression is used at the end of many musical phrases, so you will recognize its sound. You can hear some examples on the website.

A dominant 7th chord is built on the fifth degree of the scale, or dominant, and has four notes that are a 3rd apart from each other. Each note is given a number that describes its relationship to the root (1st note) of the chord. For example, in G major, the fifth degree of the scale is D and the notes of the dominant 7th chord are D (root), F♯ (3rd), A (5th), and C (7th).

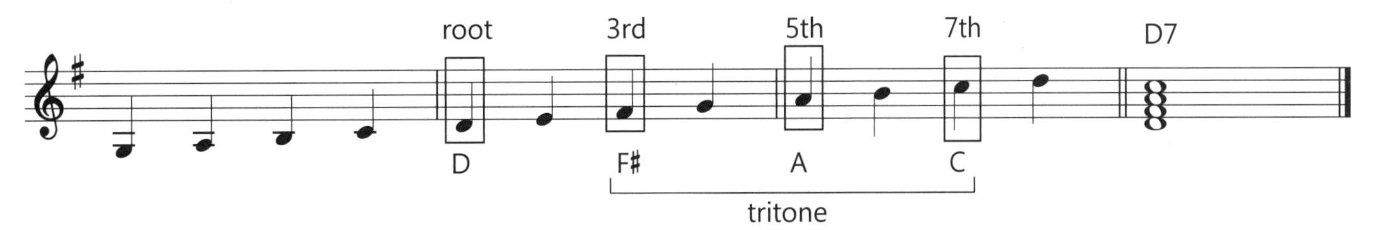

All dominant 7th chords contain a diminished 5th, or tritone, between the third and seventh notes. This interval is dissonant and uncomfortable to listen to—our desire for it to be resolved drives the movement from dominant to tonic. On the violin it's difficult to play chords so we arpeggiate the notes instead (i.e. play them one at a time). Try out a couple of dominant 7th arpeggios below.

One-octave dominant 7th arpeggios in G and C

- Listen carefully to the tuning of the 2nd-finger notes.
- Notice that each arpeggio starts on the fifth degree of the scale (the dominant) and resolves to the tonic.

Dominant 7th arpeggio in the key of G, starting on D

Dominant 7th arpeggio in the key of C, starting on G

TRY...

Can you work out how to play a one-octave dominant 7th arpeggio in the key of D, starting on an open A?

Little Laendler  

Can you spot the dominant 7th arpeggio patterns in this piece? Keep your 2nd finger nimble as it moves between its high and low positions. Play the crotchets with a slightly staccato bow-stroke.

Julian Rowlands (b. 1960)

Fingering notes an augmented 4th or diminished 5th (tritone) apart 

Notes a tritone apart (see page 5) are fingered in a similar way to notes a semitone apart: they can either be played using adjacent fingers, placing the finger for the second note close to the finger for the first note, or using the same finger for both notes. When using the same finger we can't slide it between the notes because we have to change string as well, so we have to 'hop' it between its low and high positions as we change strings, taking care to minimize disruption to the melodic line. Try playing the following intervals:

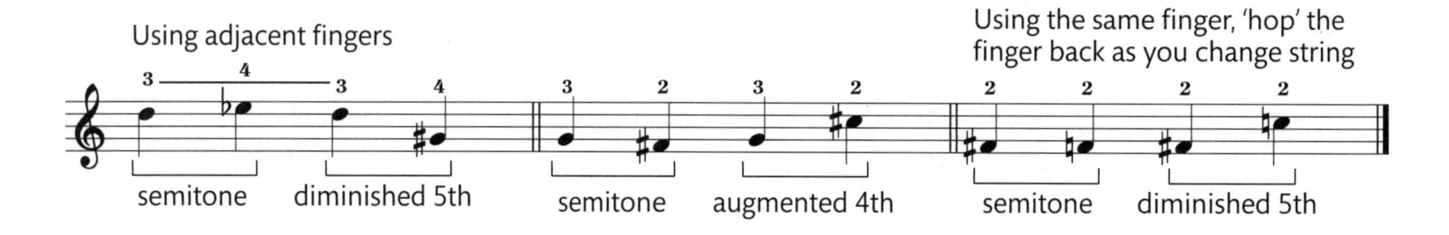

Theme from *The 'Trout' Quintet*  

Look out for the diminished 5th intervals in bars 7 and 11. Slide your 4th finger up a semitone to play the A in bar 8. Play the separate crotchets with light, staccato bow-strokes. Keep your left-hand fingers really rhythmic in bar 3.

TRY...

In bar 11 an alternative, smoother fingering would be to play the two crotchet C sharps with your 3rd finger, the G natural with your 2nd finger, and the final C sharp quaver with your 2nd finger. To do this, your 3rd finger will need to reach back a semitone into a new, lower position–this movement should be made from the base knuckle without changing the position of your hand. Have a go at this fingering and use it instead of the marked fingering if you find it easier.

9 MINOR SCALES AND ARPEGGIOS

The harmonic minor 

- The notes of the harmonic minor scale are the same as those of the natural minor scale (see Book 1, chapter 18), except that the seventh degree (note) is raised by one semitone, making an **augmented 2nd** interval between the sixth and seventh degrees of the scale. This sharpened 7th is indicated by an accidental preceding the note.
- The pattern of intervals in a harmonic minor scale is: **tone**, **semitone**, **tone**, **tone**, **semitone**, **augmented 2nd**, **semitone**.
- The sharpened seventh note of the harmonic minor scale leads to the eighth note (the tonic) in the same way as the seventh note of the major scale does. This is very important in minor-key harmony, hence the name of the scale.
- The augmented 2nd gives the harmonic minor scale a rather mysterious, 'eastern' quality to its sound. Listen to the recording of the D harmonic minor scale on the website and try singing it before you play it.
- Play each scale with even notes (as shown on page 30) as well as with the 'long tonic' rhythm shown below.
- Listen carefully to the tuning of the minor 3rd interval between the first two notes of the arpeggios.

One-octave D harmonic minor scale and arpeggio

The key signature of D minor contains one flat: B♭. D minor is the **relative minor** of F major.

One-octave A harmonic minor scale and arpeggio

A minor has no sharps or flats in its key signature. A minor is the **relative minor** of C major.

One-octave G harmonic minor scale and arpeggio

The key signature of G minor contains two flats: B♭ and E♭. G minor is the relative minor of B♭ major.

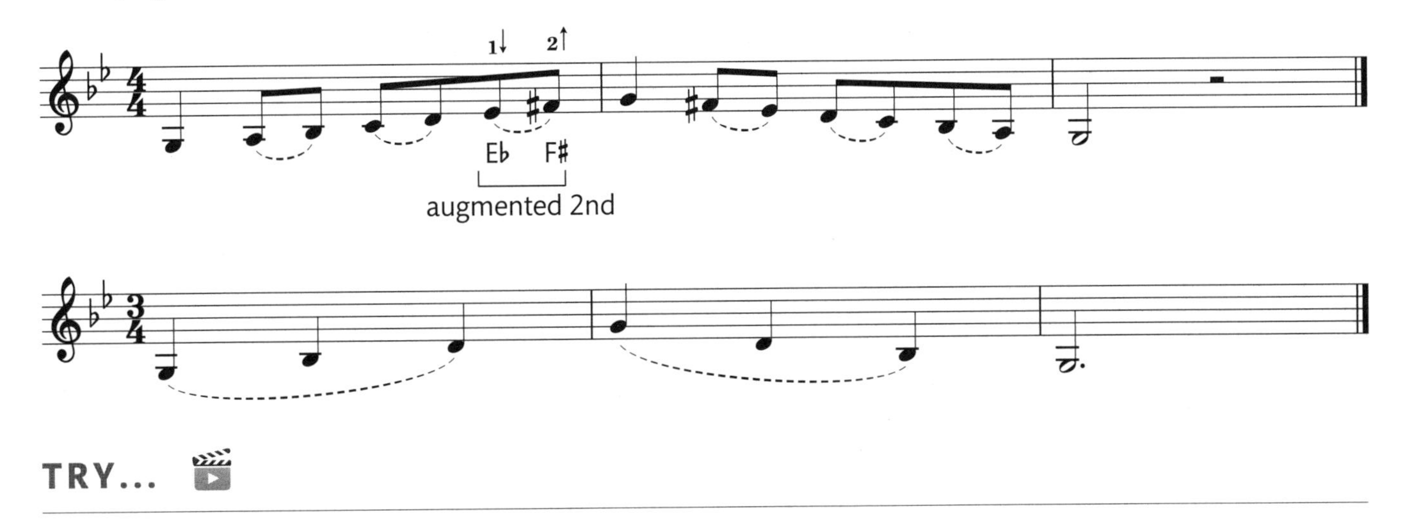

TRY...

Now try playing a two-octave G harmonic minor scale and arpeggio, from open G up to 2nd-finger G on the E string, and a two-octave A harmonic minor scale and arpeggio starting on 1st-finger A on the G string. You'll find notation and demonstration tracks on the website.

Look out for augmented 2nds and the sharpened seventh degree of the harmonic minor scale in the next pieces.

A Ya Zain

This piece is based on the D harmonic minor scale. Draw a circle around each of the augmented 2nd intervals.

Theme from Symphony No. 40

*This piece is in G minor—which note is the sharpened 7th degree of the scale? Play the separate **p** crotchets in the middle to upper half of the bow with short, light staccato strokes and the **f** crotchets with heavier staccato strokes. Look out for the diminished 5th interval between C♮ and F♯ in bars 10, 12, 29, and 31. This interval can either be fingered using the 2nd finger for both notes, hopping the finger forward to play the F♯, as marked, or by reaching back with the 3rd finger to play the F♯, as described on page 53.*

Wolfgang Amadeus Mozart (1756-91)

TRY...

When you can play this piece well at the marked tempo, try going a bit faster—it's often performed at around 𝅗𝅥 = 112. See how close you can get to this tempo!

Theme from 'Summer' (First Movement)  

This piece should be played with a languid sound, as if drowsy from the heat; try playing without vibrato and slightly sul tasto. *Can you spot the two descending D harmonic minor scale patterns? Look out for the diminished 5th interval between G and C♯ in bars 10–11.*

Antonio Vivaldi (1678–1741)

The melodic minor 

- In the melodic minor both the sixth and seventh notes are raised by a semitone on the way up the scale. On the way back down the scale reverts to the natural minor, with the sixth and seventh notes lowered back down by a semitone so that they are played according to the key signature.
- This results in melodies that are more natural to sing, or more 'melodic', with the notes following the direction of the melody. Try singing the D melodic minor scale below.
- Play each scale with even notes (see page 30) as well as with the 'long tonic' rhythm shown below.
- Arpeggios are the same for the harmonic and melodic minor, since the sixth and seventh degrees of the scale are not included in the arpeggio.

One-octave D melodic minor scale

One-octave A melodic minor scale

One-octave G melodic minor scale

Look out for the sharpened sixth and seventh notes of the melodic minor scale in the next two pieces.

Ballade Op. 118, No. 3

Track 40

Play this piece with a big sound and lots of vibrato. Use long martelé *bow-strokes to play the accented notes. Have a careful look at the fingering in bars 19–21—remember that A♭ and G♯ are enharmonic equivalents (i.e. the same note).*

Johannes Brahms (1833–97)

Andantino in Modo di Canzona from Symphony No. 4

Track 41

Play this piece with a gentle sound and long, flowing bow-strokes. Watch out for the slurred perfect 5ths in bars 1, 9, 13, 15, and 17. Practise these bars slowly to get a really legato sound.

Pyotr Ilyich Tchaikovsky (1840–93)

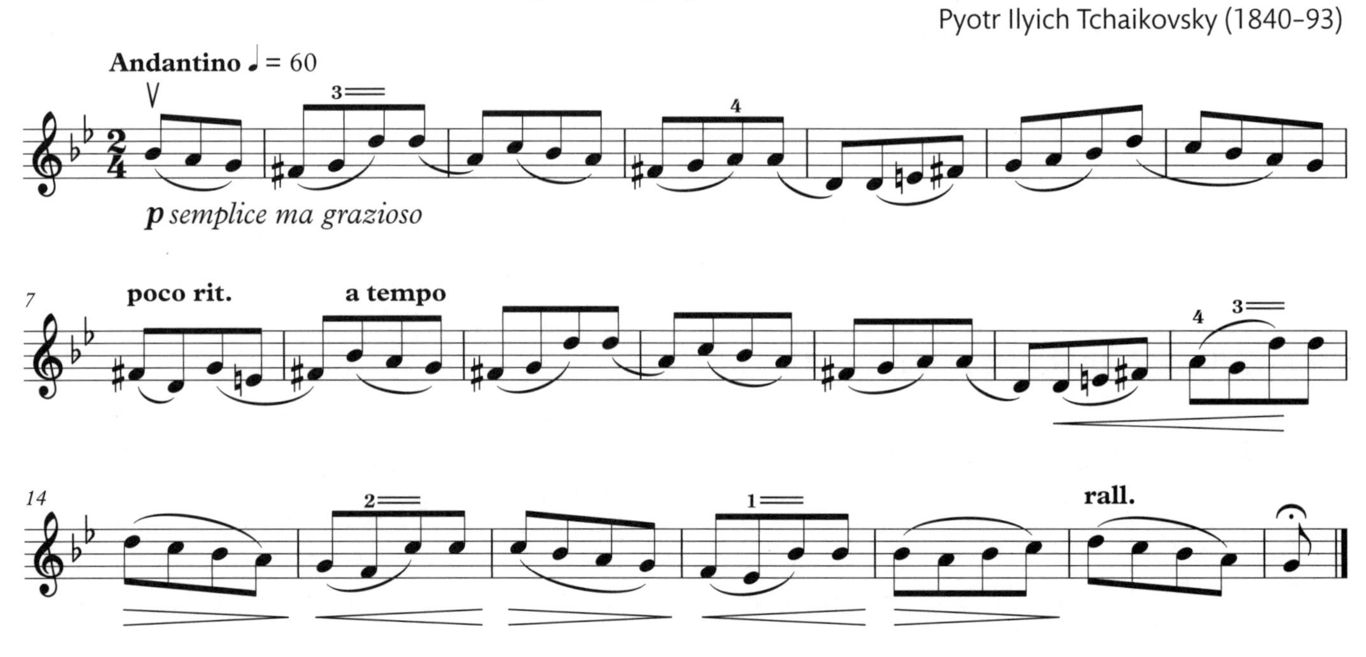

Is it a major or a minor key?

Each key signature is used for two different keys: a major key and the relative minor of that key, so you can't tell if a piece is major or minor just by looking at the key signature. For example, the Minuet below could be in either B♭ major or G minor. Here's how to work out whether a piece is in a major or a minor key:

- Look at the key signature and check the circle of 5ths (page 100) to find out the relative major and minor keys for that key signature.
- Are there any accidentals in the piece? If so, this is often an indication that it's in a minor key. For example, the Minuet contains F♯ and E♮ accidentals, which are the raised sixth and seventh degrees of the melodic minor scale.
- Look at the first and last notes: pieces often start on the first, third, or fifth degree of the scale, and usually finish on the tonic (the first degree of the scale). The Minuet starts on B♭, which is the third degree of the G minor scale and also the tonic of the B♭ major scale, but it ends on a G, so it is in the key of G minor.

Minuet in G minor 

Play this piece in the middle to upper half of the bow, using light, staccato bow-strokes for the crotchets, with a slight emphasis on the first beat of each bar. Be sure to move the whole arm as you cross the strings in bars 4–5 and 20–21, keeping your elbow level with your bowing hand.

Johann Sebastian Bach (1685–1750)

Changing between major and minor keys

- Many pieces of music are written with contrasting sections in major or minor keys.
- Pieces that start in a major key most commonly change to either the relative minor or the parallel (tonic) minor and, in a minor key, to the relative major or the parallel (tonic) major.
- Relative major and minor keys share a key signature but have different tonic notes (i.e. the scales start on different notes).
- Parallel (tonic) major and minor keys have the same tonic note (i.e. the scales start on the same note) but different key signatures. A change of key signature usually occurs when a piece of music changes from major to parallel (tonic) minor or vice versa.

El Choclo

Track 42

This famous Argentine tango is in the key of G minor with a contrasting section in G major, the parallel major key, starting at bar 25. The first section should be played marcato*, which means 'marked'—use a short, almost* martelé *bow-stroke on the accented notes to achieve this. In contrast, the section starting at bar 17 should be more legato and romantic, and the section from bar 25 should be played with a lighter bow-stroke for a more playful sound.*

Ángel Villoldo (1861–1919)

Ma Bella Bimba

This piece starts in B♭ major, has a contrasting middle section in the relative minor (G minor) starting at bar 9, and then returns to the home key of B♭ major on the D.S. Listen to the recording without looking at the music and see if you can hear the key change. Keep the bow-strokes light for a sweet, playful sound.

Italian trad.

10 NEW BOWING TECHNIQUES PART 3

Lifted staccato up-bow strokes

Up until now you have played staccato bow-strokes on the string, but staccato can also be played 'off the string' using lifted bow-strokes. Lifted staccato up-bow strokes sound like a little jump in the music, and are often used to move the bow to the lower half or heel before playing a longer note, for example when a staccato crotchet is followed by a minim.

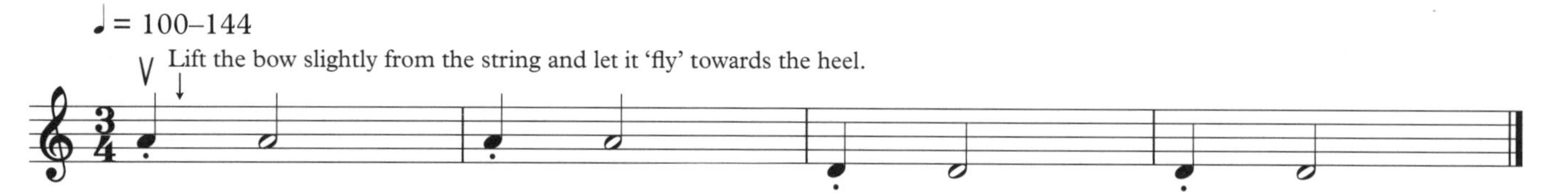

- Play a short staccato up-bow crotchet starting in the upper half or the middle of the bow. At the end of the note, instead of stopping the bow on the string, use the momentum of the arm to lift the bow off the string and let it 'fly' towards the heel. Think of an aeroplane taking off, but keep the bow as close to the strings as you can.
- Land the bow back down on the string near the heel ready to play the minim, controlling the landing carefully and keeping your right-hand fingers and wrist flexible.
- Play the minim with a long down-bow stroke so that the bow returns to its starting point, then play the next bar in the same way.
- Say '*ta-taa*' to get an idea of how each bar should be articulated.

Menuetto from Symphony No. 36

Track 44

Start this piece at around the middle of the bow. Play the staccato crotchets in bars 1–3, 10–16, and 24–6 with lifted up-bow strokes, and the linked staccato up-bow crotchets on the string in the usual way (see page 12). Play the first note of each bar full length and with a slight emphasis to give the music a stately and refined character.

Gypsy Waltz

Track 45

Use lifted staccato up-bow strokes in bars 9–12 and 17–20. Start the staccato up-bow strokes at around the middle of the bow and land the bow back on the string near the heel. Open-string bowing practice will help with this (see page 6).

RS

Circular bowing and forearm rotation

When the bow is crossing rapidly to and fro between two adjacent strings, making the string-crossing movement with the whole arm from the shoulder can be too slow and heavy. In these situations a slightly different string-crossing technique known as 'circular' bowing is often used: angle the bow so that it's level with both strings, leave your elbow in this position, and lift or drop your forearm just enough to move the bow from one string to the other. This technique works best with short strokes in the middle of the bow.

- Place the middle of the bow on the E and A strings so that it touches both strings. Make sure your elbow is at the same level as your bowing hand.
- Keeping your upper arm still, slightly lift your forearm so that the bow touches only the A string, and then lower it so that it touches only the E string. Make this vertical bow movement as small as you can—just enough to clear the adjacent string. Repeat a few times.
- Now repeat the exercise, this time playing a short down-bow stroke (approx. two inches) on the A string, followed by a short up-bow on the E string. Start slowly, making gaps between the notes, then speed up and join the notes together. Can you feel your right hand making small, clockwise circles?
- Now go the other way, playing down-bows on the E string and up-bows on the A string—can you feel your hand making small, anti-clockwise circles?
- Repeat on the D and A strings and the G and D strings.

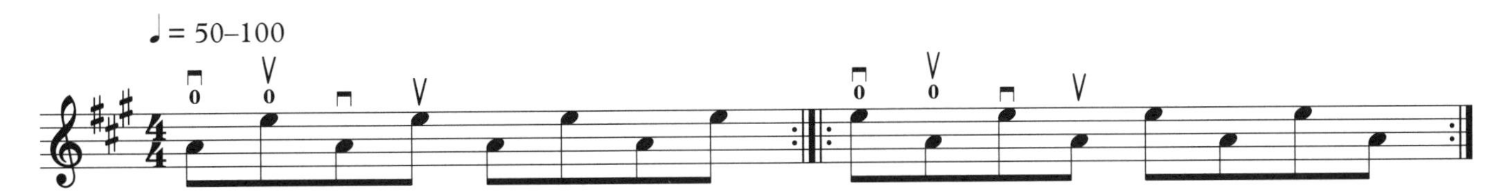

Exercise: Drawing circles

Play this exercise with circular bowing, using short strokes, at around the middle of the bow. Use open E unless marked with a 4th finger. Start slowly and gradually speed up. Feel your forearm making small clockwise, circular movements. Try not to touch the E string with your left-hand fingers—keep them a little more upright than usual so that they arch over the string.

String-Crossing Study

Play bars 17–19 and 21–3 with circular bowing in the middle of the bow, leaving your fingers down on the E string as shown. Your forearm will make small anti-clockwise, circular movements as you cross the strings. Other string crossings should be made in the usual way, moving the whole arm as a unit from the shoulder.

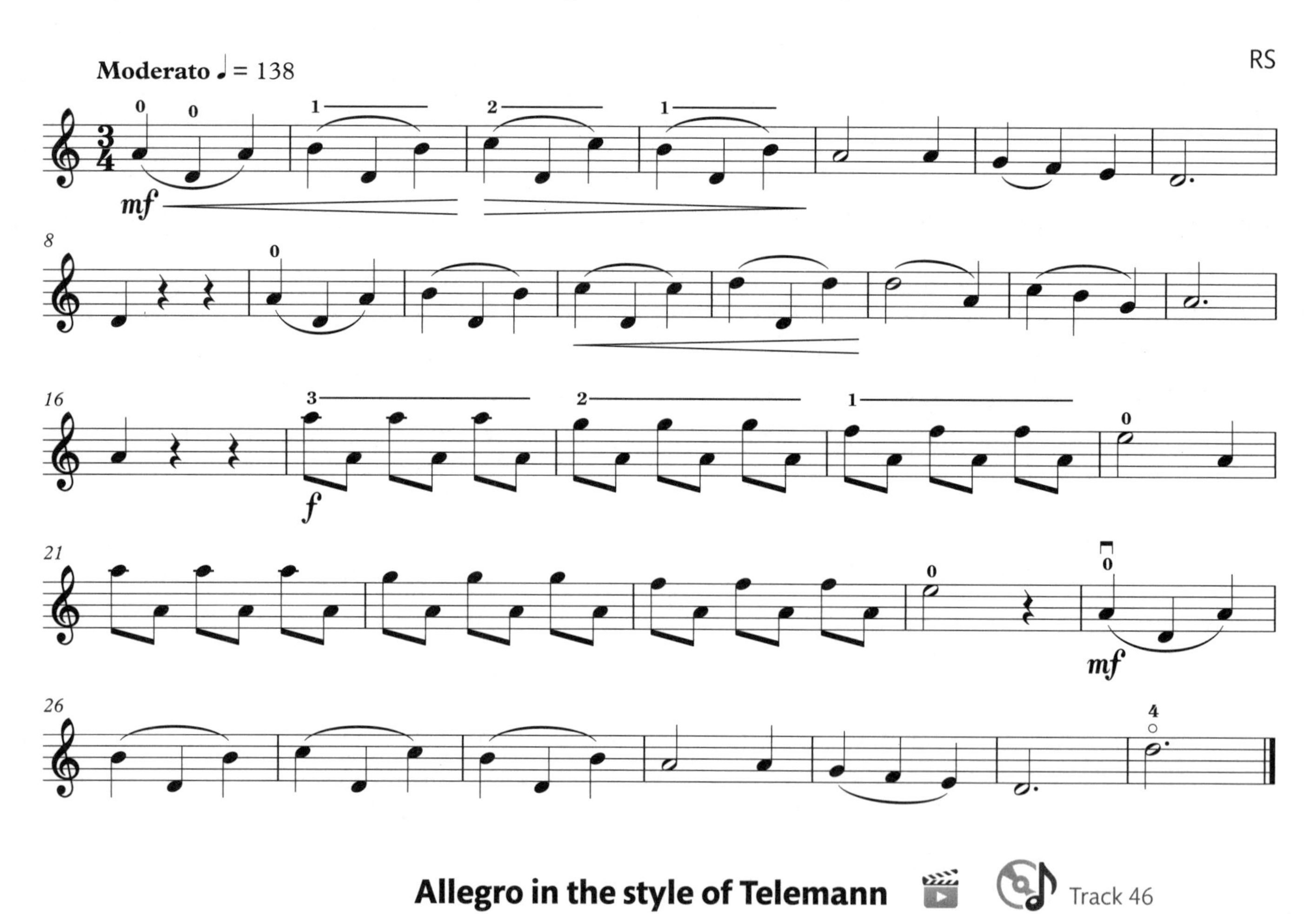

Allegro in the style of Telemann

Track 46

The crotchets in this piece should be played with a slightly staccato bow-stroke. Use lifted staccato up-bow strokes on the crotchets at the beginning of bars 26 and 28, and use circular bowing in bars 13–16 and 42–5 (see Technical Tip opposite).

TECHNICAL TIP

- Say the word 'butter' to get the feel of the rhythm in bars 13–16 and 42–5 of 'Allegro in the style of Telemann', then practise the bowing for these bars on open strings, as shown below.
- Play in the middle of the bow using a faster, accented bow-stroke on the quavers and a slower bow-stroke on the dotted crotchets so that you're using about the same amount of bow on both notes.
- Notice that the circular movement of the forearm is anti-clockwise in bars 13–16 and clockwise in bars 42–5.

11 QUAVER TRIPLETS AND SWING QUAVERS

IN THIS CHAPTER you'll learn two new rhythmic ideas: quaver triplets and swing quavers, both of which will probably sound familiar to you.

Triplets

A triplet is a group of three equal notes with the same total duration as two notes of the same kind. Triplets are written with a small '3' above or below the beam, or in a bracket.

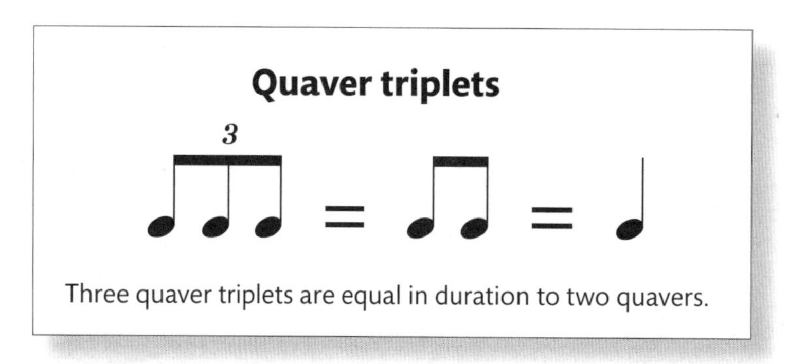

Three quaver triplets are equal in duration to two quavers.

Exercise 1: Clapping and playing quaver triplets

- Practise clapping, then playing, quaver triplets along to your metronome (♩ = 60). Say 'one-and-a, two-and-a, three-and-a, four-and-a' to help you subdivide each crotchet beat into three equal parts. Play on any note.
- Clap, then play, the rhythms below. When this feels easy try playing at faster and slower tempos.

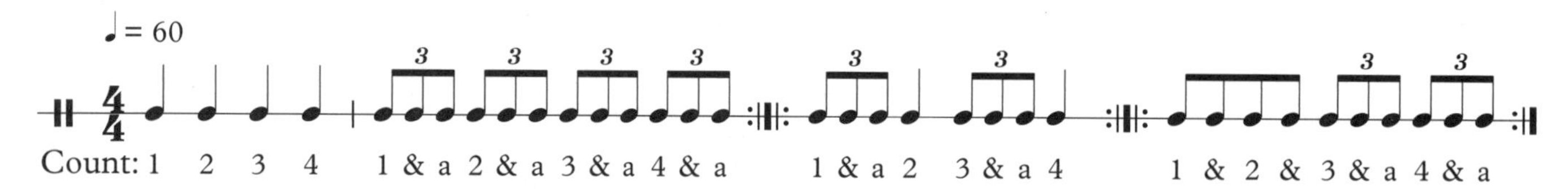

Exercise 2: Call and response

Work through the call and response track on the website, echoing back the rhythms in the gaps.

Exercise 3: What shall we do with the drunken sailor?

Play this triplet variation of the famous sea shanty. Sing the words to help with the rhythm.

Exercise 4: Playing scales with quaver triplets

- Put a slight accent on the first of each group of triplets. Notice that the groups of triplets start alternately with down-bows and up-bows.
- Practise at slower and faster tempos. Try playing some of your other scales with triplets.

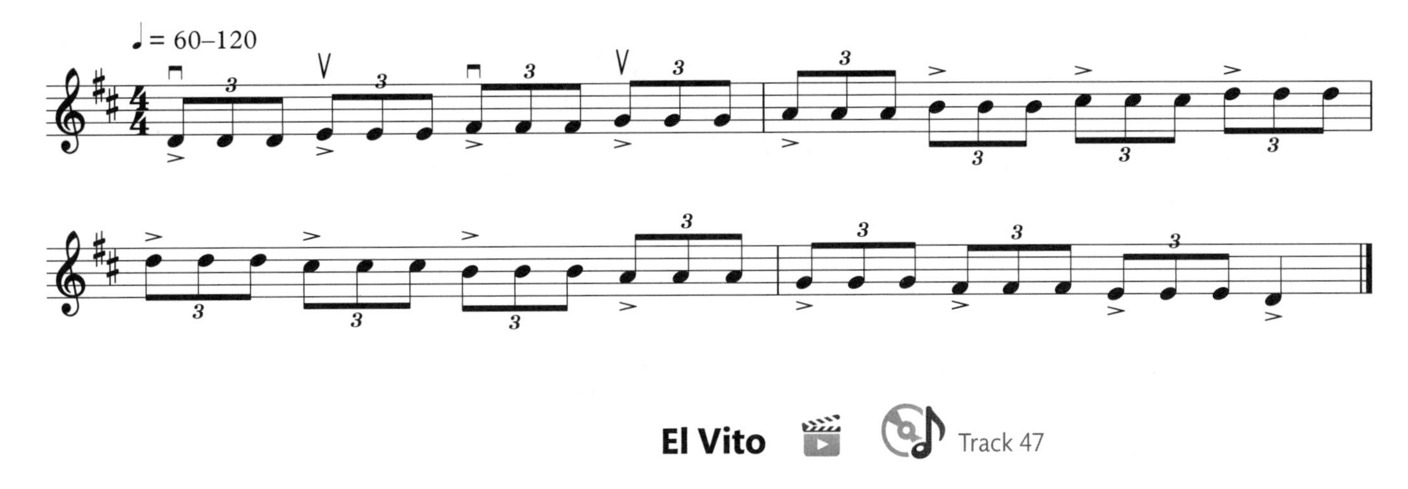

El Vito Track 47

Try playing this haunting Spanish melody with long, but quite light, bow-strokes to create a mysterious sound.

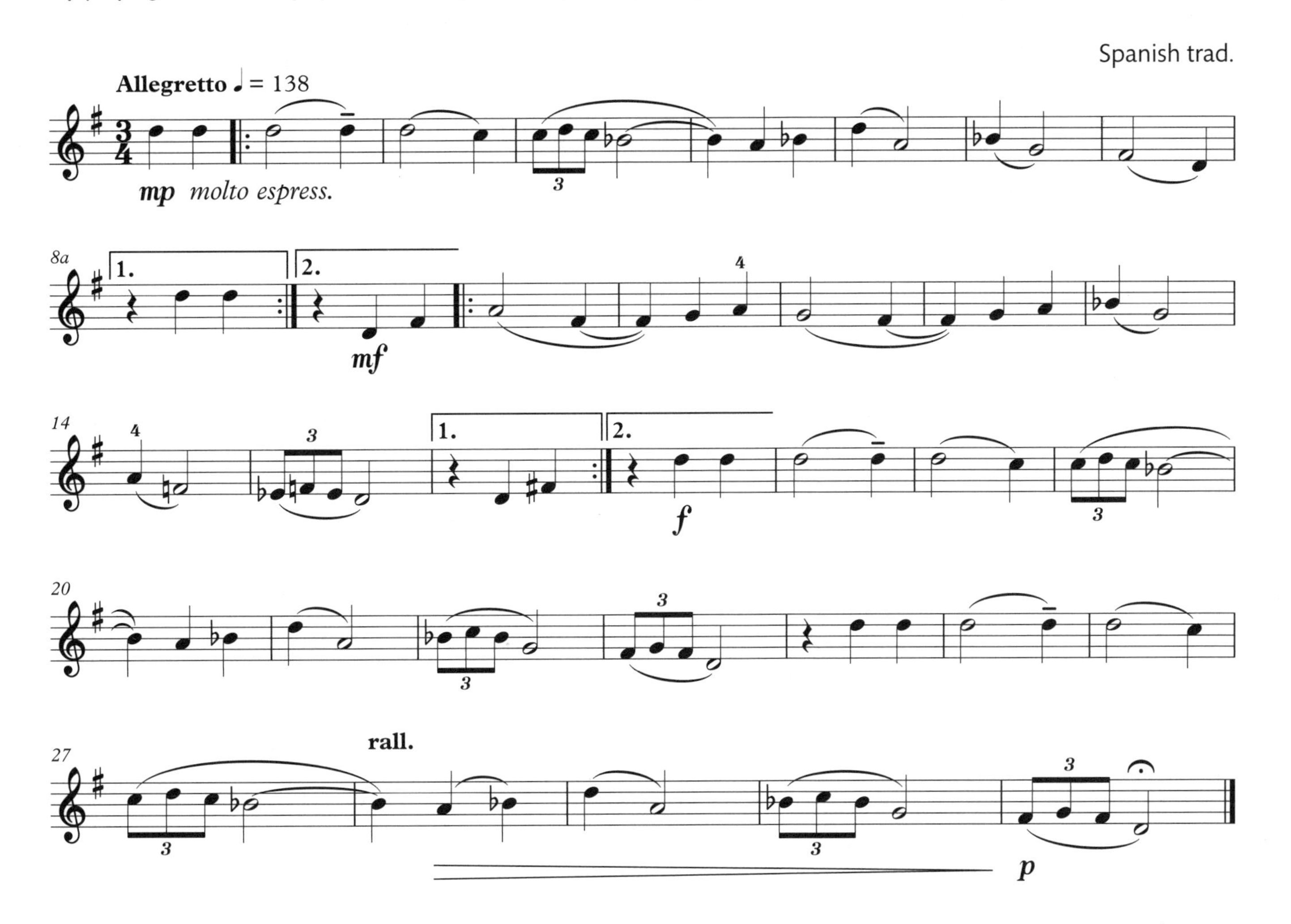

Waltz from *Lyrische Stücke*

Track 48

Grieg was a Norwegian composer, and his music was often inspired by native folk music. Look up the traditional hardanger *fiddle—it's an amazing instrument! Play the staccato crotchets in bars 5, 9, 23, and 27 with slightly lifted staccato up-bow strokes. Look out for the key change to A major at bar 37 and in the coda.*

Edvard Grieg (1843–1907)

Allegro moderato ♩ = 112

Añoranza

Track 49

This piece by the Spanish composer Granados is based on a traditional Spanish folk song. Clap the rhythm of the melody along to a metronome before you play it.

Enrique Granados (1867–1916)

Swing quavers

Swing is the uneven long-short rhythm commonly used to play pairs of quavers in jazz and jazz-influenced music. It is written as even quavers but played as an uneven triplet rhythm:

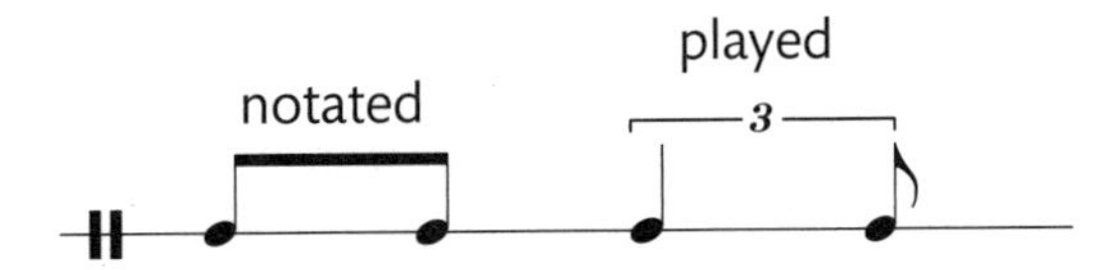

Exercise 1: Clapping and playing swing quavers

- Practise clapping swing quavers along to your metronome (♩ = 100), or along to the swing-rhythm backing track on the website.
- Now play swing quavers on a single note in the upper half of the bow, again along to the backing track.
- Try to make them sound relaxed—take care not to turn the triplet into a ♩.♪ rhythm.
- Listen to recordings by famous jazz violinists such as Eddie South, Stéphane Grappelli, and Big Bill Broonzy.

Exercise 2: Swinging the D blues scale

Play the D blues scale below with a swing rhythm. Play with and without slurs.

Exercise 3: Improvising a blues tune

- Try improvising a 12-bar blues tune along to the blues backing track on the website using the notes of the D blues scale.
- Pick a simple rhythm, for example the rhythm of the words 'I'm swinging blues quavers' (♩ ♫♩ ♫), and clap it along to the backing track with a swing feel.

- Now play long, four-beat notes along to the backing track, using just the notes F♯, F, and E. Start on F♯ and change note when the one you're playing sounds wrong against the backing track—you'll need to listen carefully to hear which note fits best. When this feels easy, try playing your swing rhythm instead of some of the long notes.
- Try adding more notes from the scale and try out some different rhythms.

Sliding up to notes

To play a slide up to a note, such as in bar 2 of 'Bluegrass Waltz', reach back about a semitone with the finger and slide it up the string to the desired pitch. Start by playing a slow slide up from the lower note, as shown below, then make the slide quicker and reduce the pressure of the finger on the string at the beginning of the slide so that there isn't an obvious starting note.

Bluegrass Waltz

Play the pairs of quavers in this piece with a long-short swing rhythm, and triplet quavers with equal-length notes. An occasional 'bluesy' slide (see 'Sliding up to notes' above) will sound good—a few are suggested, but also try some of your own.

RS

Greenmarket Square

Track 51

This piece is in the style of South African township swing music. Practise clapping the rhythm along to the recording. This piece sounds good with the occasional slide up to a note—try this out in a few places. You could also try playing bars 21–3 an octave higher for a more dramatic effect.

RS

12 DOUBLE STOPPING

DOUBLE STOPPING MEANS playing two adjacent strings simultaneously. Although the term suggests that the strings are to be fingered (stopped), in practice one or both strings may be open. When you've worked through this chapter, have a go at tuning your violin by playing two strings together. See the website for guidance on this.

Playing two open strings together

Exercise 1: Full bow-strokes 

- Angle your bowing arm so that the bow rests on both strings.
- Play the two strings together with a slow, steady bow-stroke. The aim is to get a clear, focused, even sound without any bulges, and with both strings ringing clearly throughout the bow-stroke. Make changes of bow direction as smooth as you can.

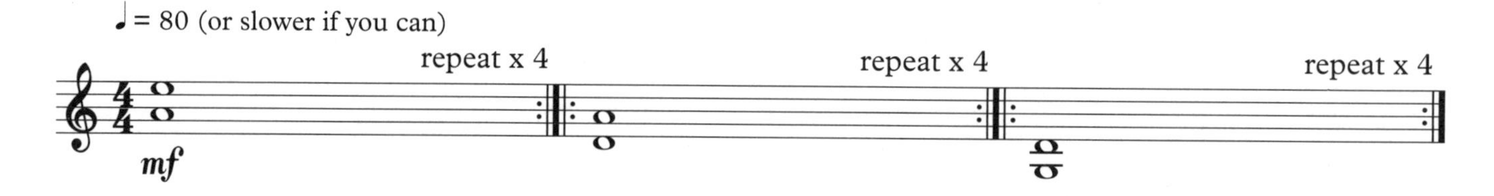

TECHNICAL TIP

You don't need to use any extra pressure with the bow when playing two strings at the same time. Keep your right hand relaxed and flexible and make sure your bowing arm is angled so that the bow touches both the strings. Think about how to control the sound in different parts of the bow: in the lower half, you'll need to balance more of the weight of the bow in your hand, especially at quieter dynamics, and in the upper half at louder dynamics you'll need to use more arm weight to get a clear, full sound.

Exercise 2: Double stop rhythms

Now play double stops on open strings with different rhythms. Practise on all the strings, in the lower half, middle, and upper half of the bow. Make up some rhythms of your own.

Playing an open string with a stopped note

Exercise: Double stopping a major scale with open strings

- Play a D major scale with your bow angled so that it touches both the D and the A strings at the same time. Play very slowly at first, then gradually increase the tempo.
- Make sure the stopping finger doesn't touch the open string above or below—the open string should ring out clearly. Where the lower note is the stopped note, play more on your fingertips than usual so that your fingers 'arch' over the open string.
- Listen carefully and adjust your finger position if the tuning doesn't sound right.
- Repeat with one-octave G and A major scales.

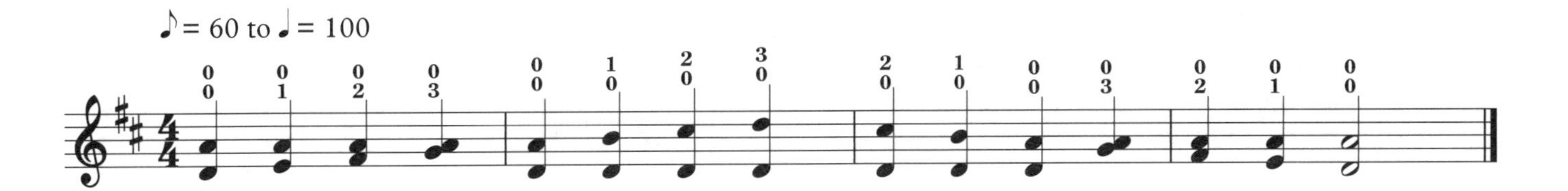

Old Time Fiddle is a genre of folk music from the USA. When stopping the lower string remember to keep your fingers arched and to play a little more on your fingertips than usual, so that the open string above rings out clearly.

Old Time Fiddle Tune trad.

Energetically 𝅗𝅥 = 69

f

5 **Fine**

9 *mf* *cresc.*

13 **1.** *f* **2.** **D.C. al Fine** *f*

Transylvanian Stick Dance

This piece is in the style of a Romanian folk dance. 'Pesante' means 'heavily'—make a big sound and use plenty of bow in the forte sections.

TECHNICAL TIP

The intervals in bars 12 and 13 of 'Transylvanian Stick Dance' are a major 6th and a minor 6th respectively. Play these intervals slowly as double stops while listening very carefully—notice that a tiny adjustment to your 1st-finger position makes a big difference to how well in tune the interval sounds.

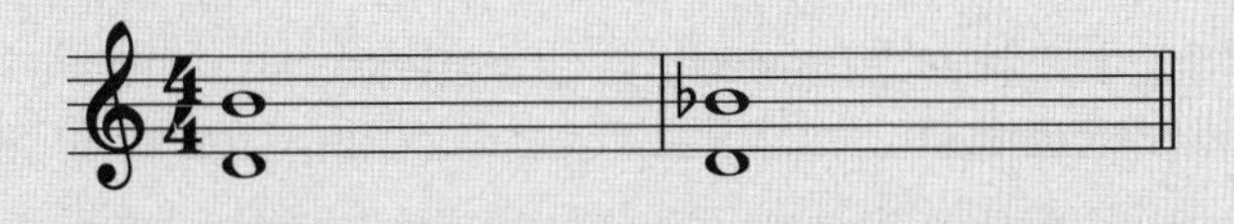

Hungarian Folk Dance  Track 54

Practise the bowing on open strings, then play each double stop slowly, listening very carefully to your intonation. Watch out for the change to stopping the lower string in bar 6.

Hungarian trad.

13 CHROMATIC SCALES

A CHROMATIC SCALE is a twelve-note scale that contains all the semitones of the octave; the notes in a chromatic scale are all a semitone apart. The word 'chromatic' comes from the Greek word *chroma*, meaning colour, and chromatic notes are traditionally considered to 'colour' or 'shade' the diatonic notes (the notes defined by the key signature). Chromatic scales are usually notated using sharps when ascending; when descending, the sharpened notes are often replaced with their **enharmonic** equivalents so that only flats are used.

One-octave chromatic scales 

- The 1st and 2nd fingers slide up or down a semitone between the notes. Try not to make these slides audible—move your finger at the same time as you change bow direction.
- The 3rd and 4th fingers play just one note each. The 4th finger is always played in the low position, a semitone below the open string above.
- It's easy to go flat or sharp in chromatic scales, so be extra aware of your intonation. Check the tuning of 3rd-finger G, D, and A with the open string below. It can also help to practise a run of four notes at a time, checking your intonation at the beginning and end of each group.
- Play the scales very slowly to start with (♪ = 60), then gradually increase the tempo (up to ♩ = 120).

Chromatic scale starting on A

The next two scales use the same fingering; try to remember it rather than write it in.

Chromatic scales starting on D and G

TRY...

When you can play these chromatic scales confidently with separate bow strokes, try adding slurs. Start by slurring two notes together, then move on to slurring groups of three then four notes.

Habanera from *Carmen*  

This famous piece is from Bizet's opera Carmen, *and is based on a descending chromatic scale.*

Georges Bizet (1838–75)

'To the Evening Star' from *Tannhäuser*

Track 56

This beautiful song is from Wagner's opera Tannhäuser. *Play with slow, smooth, controlled bow-strokes and listen very carefully to the tuning of the chromatic notes. Practise bars 26–7 slowly for intonation—make sure you reach up high enough for the 3rd-finger G♯ after playing the low 1st-finger D♯.*

Richard Wagner (1813–83)

Crotchet triplets

Three crotchet triplets are equal to the duration of two normal crotchets.

Exercise: Clapping crotchet triplets

It's important to be able to keep track of the crotchet pulse when playing crotchet triplets. When triplet and duplet rhythms are played at the same time this this is known as a 'three against two' rhythm.

- Set your metronome to a steady crotchet pulse (♩ = 63) and tap your foot along with it.
- At the same time, count groups of six triplet quavers (subdividing the crotchet pulse into three equal parts). The metronome clicks and your foot taps on the first and fourth of each group of six quavers: **1**, 2, 3, **4**, 5, 6.
- Stop tapping your foot. Continue counting the triplet quavers out loud along to the metronome and now clap on the first, third, and fifth of each group: **1**, 2, **3**, 4, **5**, 6. You are clapping crotchet triplets along to a crotchet pulse. Take care not to speed up or slow down the triplet quaver pulse—the first and fourth triplet quavers should still coincide with the metronome click.
- Alternate between tapping the crotchet pulse and clapping crotchet triplets, while continuing to count the triplet quavers.
- When this feels easy, try counting, clapping, and tapping all at the same time. This takes a bit of practice but isn't as hard as it sounds!
- Finally, stop counting the triplet quavers out loud and just tap the crotchet pulse and clap triplet crotchets. You are now clapping a 'three against two' rhythm. It can help to think of the words '**nice cup** of **tea**' while you do this.

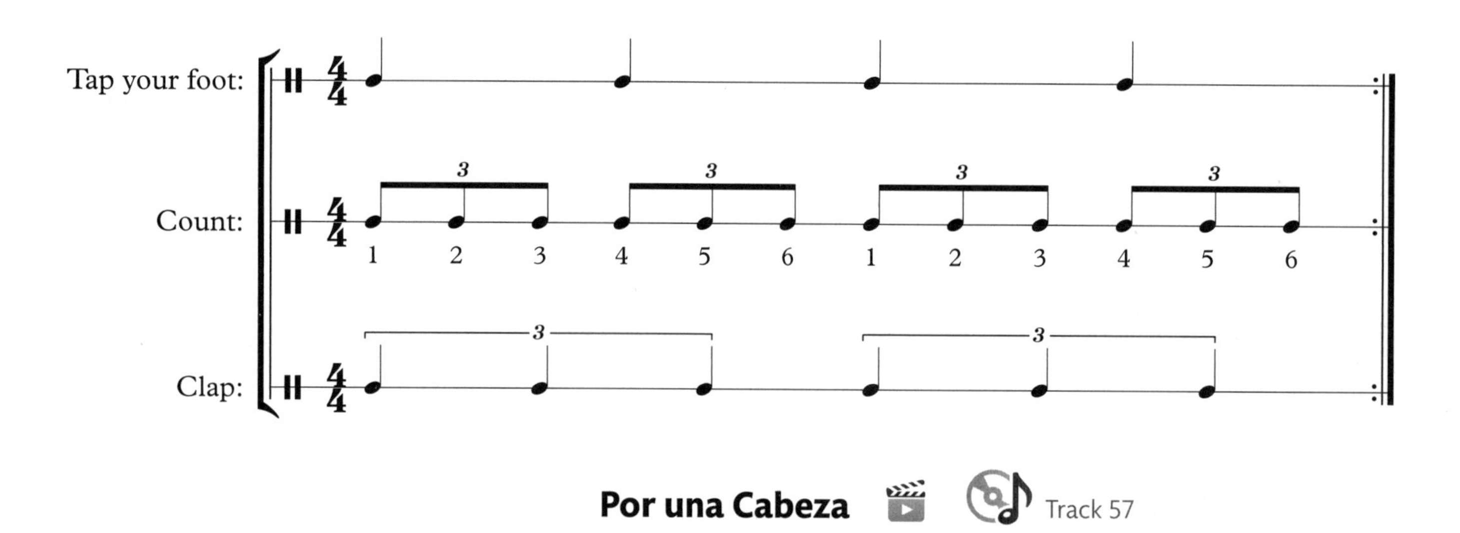

Por una Cabeza

Track 57

'Por una Cabeza' is one of the most famous Argentine tangos. The lyrics say that 'life is like a horse race where you always lose by a short head'! Sing the words 'Por una Cabeza' along to the recording in bars 17–20 to get the feel of the crotchet triplet rhythm.

Carlos Gardel (1890–1935) and
Alfredo Le Pera (1900–35)

Steady tango ♩ = 96

10
4
4
f
mp
15
f
3
3
21
3
3
27
rall.
3
3
mf
p

14 3RD POSITION

IN THIS CHAPTER you'll learn how to play higher up the neck, in 3rd position. To reach 3rd position the whole hand moves up the fingerboard and the 1st finger is placed at the same position on the string as the 3rd finger in 1st position. On the E string this gives access to notes that are above the range of 1st position, but violinists also use higher positions to avoid awkward fingerings or string crossings, or to achieve a richer, warmer tone on the lower strings.

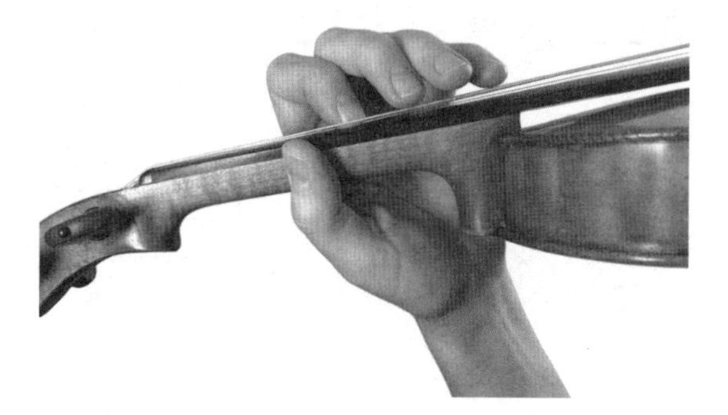

As you move higher up the fingerboard of a string instrument the vibrating length of the string becomes shorter, which means the notes gradually get closer together. You can see this if you look at the frets on a guitar. With slow practice and careful attention to intonation you'll learn to automatically adjust your finger spacing as you move up and down the instrument.

3rd-position notes and fingerings

- You'll play the following 3rd-position notes in this chapter, including three new notes on the E string.
- Fingerings are given here, but don't write them into the music unless you get really stuck.
- You'll start by playing pieces that use a 1--2--3-4 fingering pattern (with 'high' 3rd finger notes), and then go on to pieces that use a 1--2-3--4 fingering pattern (with 'low' 3rd-finger notes).

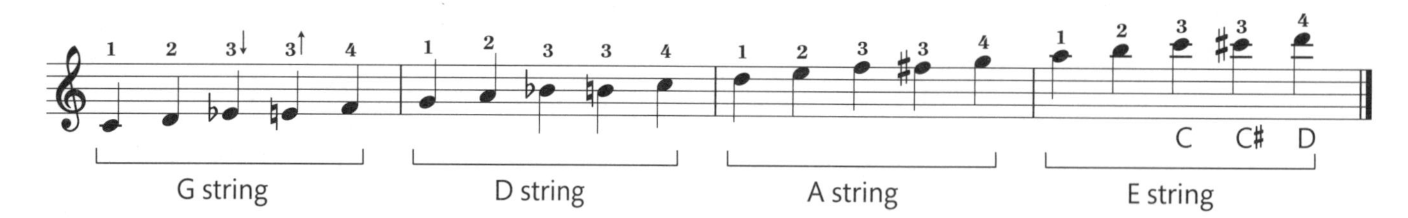

Finding 3rd position

The basic shape of the left hand in 3rd position is the same as in 1st position—the hand is just higher up the neck. Here's how to find 3rd position; repeat this on all the strings.

- Check that your violin is comfortably supported on your shoulder and that your left hand is relaxed, so that you can move your hand up and down the neck freely and without tension.
- Play G on the D string with your 3rd finger, then sing or whistle the note.
- Bend your left elbow so that your whole hand, including your thumb, slides up the fingerboard as a unit, just far enough to play the same G with your 1st finger.

- Your left wrist should be in line with the forearm, the side of your thumb (just above the top joint) should rest against the neck, and the crease at the base of the 1st finger should rest against the E-string side of the fingerboard. Your thumb should be relaxed and more or less opposite the base of the 1st finger, just as it would in 1st position.
- Your wrist will be quite close to the body of the violin, but shouldn't rest against it.
- Check the tuning of the 1st-finger G with the open G string. Listen out for the 'ringing' sound of the open string below when the 1st-finger octave is in tune. If necessary, move your whole hand up or down a little to adjust the tuning.

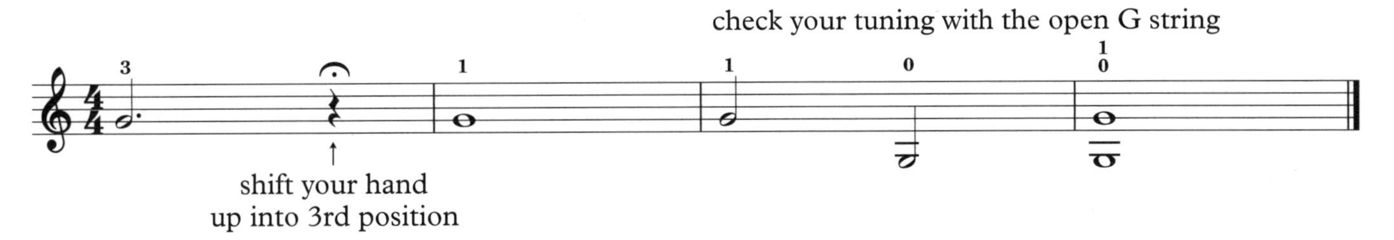

Playing Mattachins (Sword Dance) by ear in 3rd position

Reading notes in 3rd position can be confusing at first, so we'll start by playing a short piece by ear. There are backing tracks for this exercise on the website.

Play the first eight bars of 'Mattachins' in E major, using your 4th finger rather than open A, and memorize it:

Now play it in B major and memorize it. The fingering pattern is the same as in E major.

Play the tune again, starting on some other 1st-finger notes, for example: in A major, starting on 1st-finger A on the G string; in F♯ major, starting on 1st-finger F♯ on the E string; or in E♭ major, starting on 1st-finger E♭ on the D string.
When you can do this easily, have a go at playing the same tune with exactly the same fingering, but with your hand in 3rd position:

- Find 1st-finger G in 3rd position on the D string.
- Play the melody starting on this note.
- Work out the names of the notes you're playing.
- Repeat the exercise starting on 1st-finger D in 3rd position on the A string, 1st-finger C in 3rd position on the G string, and then 1st-finger A in 3rd position on the E string.
- Write out the four 3rd-position versions of the tune on manuscript paper, and write the fingering above the notes.

Repeat this idea with 'Kumbaya' or 'Stowey' (page 16). Other tunes you could try are: 'Frère Jacques', 'The Can-Can', and 'Twinkle, twinkle, little star'. Work out how to play them starting on different 1st-finger notes in 1st position, then play them starting on 1st-finger G on the D string or 1st-finger D on the A string.

Reading in 3rd position

In the next pieces the 3rd finger is in its high position and the fingering pattern is 1--2--3-4. The small notes at the beginning of each piece are to help you find your 3rd-position starting note: play them slowly while paying careful attention to your intonation and left-hand position. Make sure you know the names of the notes you're playing—say them out loud a few times.
The first piece is written out in three different keys so that you can practise reading in 3rd position on all the strings. You may find it helpful to play each version in 1st position to start with. Backing tracks in all three keys can be found on the website.

Oh! Susanna

Track 58

Stephen Foster (1826–64)

Annie Laurie

Track 59

'Restez' means 'stay in position' while playing the open As in bars 8 and 10. Practise the octave interval from 1st-finger to 4th-finger D (bars 1, 5, 13, and 15) slowly, checking your intonation with the open D string.

Scottish trad.

TRY...

Try playing 'Annie Laurie' by ear an octave lower, in 1st position, starting on 2nd-finger F♯.

Cielito Lindo

You played this piece in 1st position in Chapter 3. Now try playing it in 3rd position.

Mexican trad.

Con spirito 𝅗𝅥. = 60

TRY...

Now try playing a one-octave G major scale in 3rd position, starting on 1st-finger G on the D string.

Low 3rd finger in 3rd position

In the next three pieces the 3rd finger is in its low position and the fingering pattern is 1--2-3--4. Watch out for the semitone interval between the 2nd and 3rd fingers. Before starting the next pieces, find your 3rd-position starting note as follows:

- Play the starting note in 1st position to hear its pitch (if it's higher than a top B, play it an octave lower).
- Shift your hand into 3rd position as described on pages 80–1, check your hand position, then play the starting note, listening carefully to the tuning.

Shalom, Chaverim

Find 3rd position before starting this piece and leave your hand in 3rd position while playing the open D string at the beginning. Remember that there is a semitone between 2nd-finger A and 3rd-finger B♭ on the D string.

TRY...

'Shalom, Chaverim' sounds good accompanied by a simple drone (a long, held note or chord) made up of the notes G and D. Play this piece with a friend or your teacher and take it in turns to play the drone (play the open G and D strings at the same time, using long bow strokes). Try adding some embellishments to the melody so that it's a little different each time you play it.

Okayama Gardens

You played this piece in 1st position in Book 1—now try playing it in 3rd position. Play through the pentatonic scale shown below before you start the piece.

Japanese trad. (adapted)

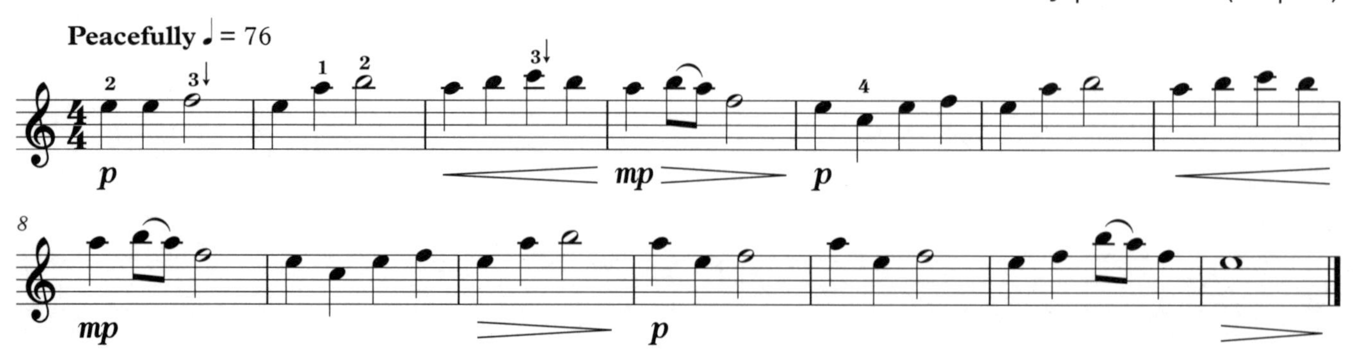

TRY...

Try improvising your own eight-bar Japanese melody in 3rd position using the notes of the pentatonic scale shown below. Start with just the first three notes of the scale and a simple rhythm, such as the rhythm of the first or fourth bar of 'Okayama Gardens'; play the notes in any order. Gradually try adding more notes from the scale and changing the rhythm. There is a backing track on the website.

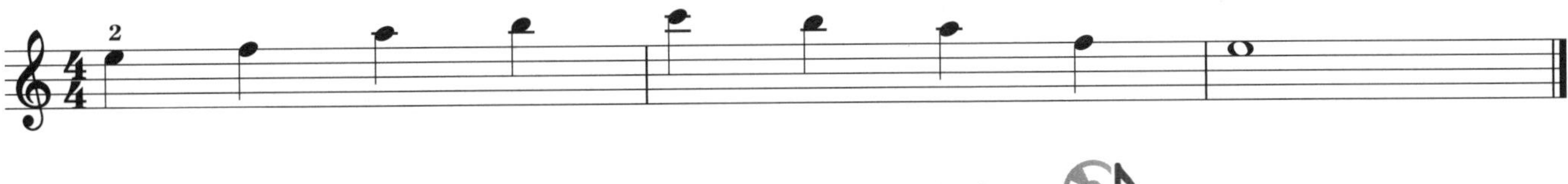

Ach, englische Schäferin

Track 62

Play this piece in 1st position to start with, then in 3rd position. When playing in 3rd position, keeping your 4th finger over the strings and ready to play will make it easier to reach the F on the G string.

German folk song
arr. Johannes Brahms (1833–97)

Playing with high and low 3rd finger in 3rd position

As in 1st position, the choice of high or low position for the fingers depends on the key signature and any accidentals, and changing string often means a change of finger position. The next exercise and pieces include high and low 3rd fingers and the 1--2--3-4 and 1--2-3--4 fingering patterns.

Exercise: Moving between 1--2--3-4 and 1--2-3--4 fingering patterns 

- Play this exercise leaving fingers down where marked, then repeat with only one finger on the string at a time, keeping unused fingers close to the strings.
- Play with and without slurs.
- Repeat on the other strings using the same fingering pattern. Sing the note names for each string.

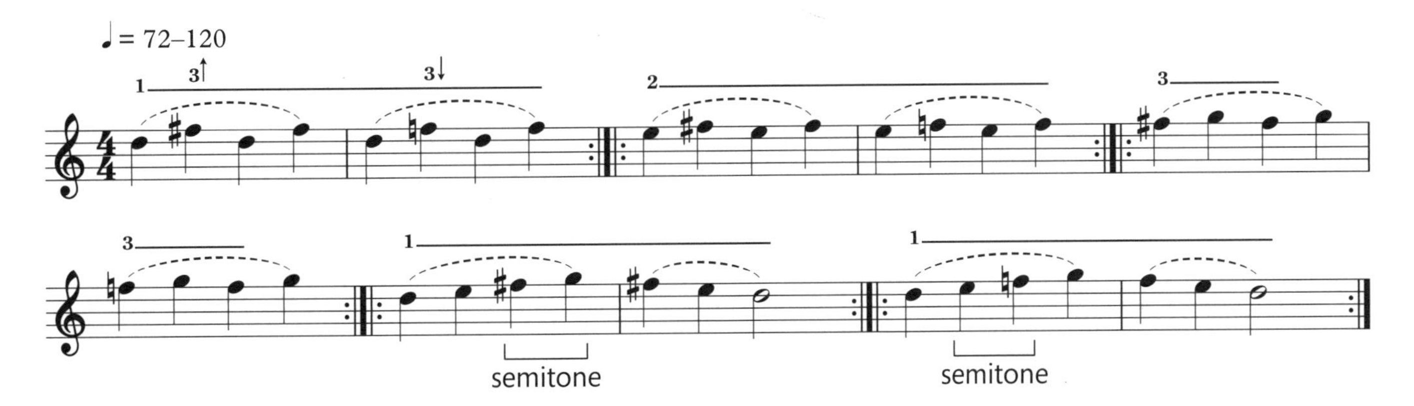

Theme from Violin Concerto

This beautiful melody is from the first movement of Beethoven's Violin Concerto. It is first played in G major, then in G minor, the parallel or tonic minor key. Remember to play the B♭s with a low 3rd finger.

Ludwig van Beethoven (1770–1827)

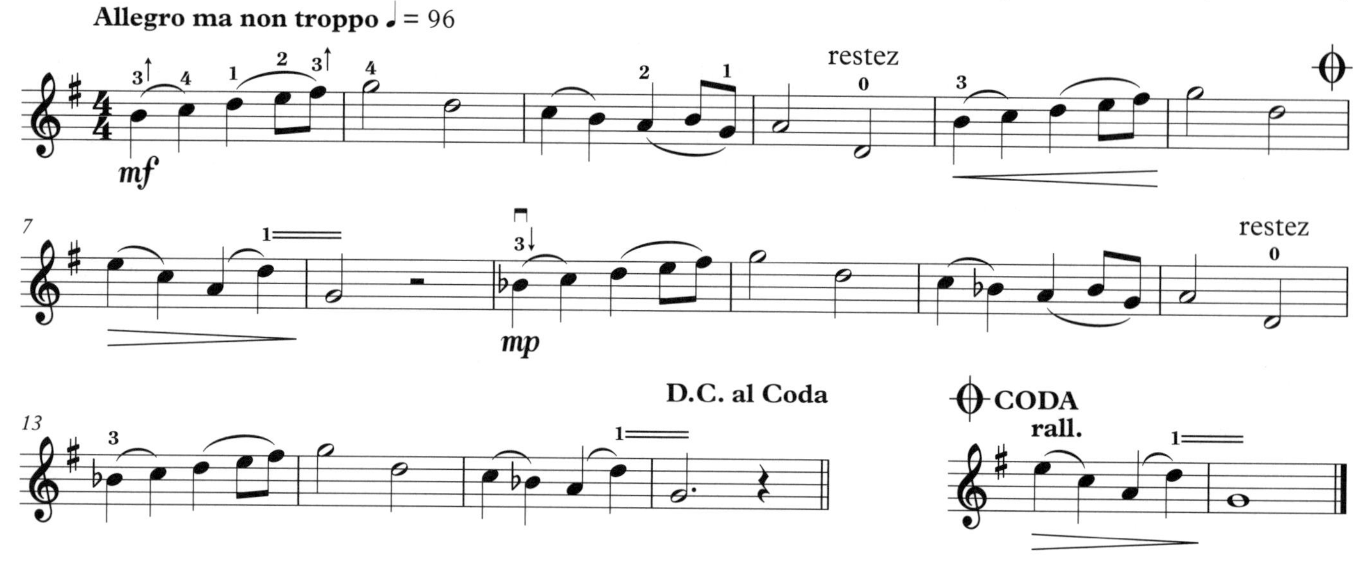

Nocturne from *A Midsummer Night's Dream*

This piece is from Mendelssohn's incidental music for the Shakespeare play. You'll play a low 3rd-finger B♭ on the D string and a high 3rd-finger E on the G string. Make sure you know where the semitone intervals are before you start playing.

Felix Mendelssohn (1809–47)

Barcarolle from *The Tales of Hoffman*  Track 65

Watch out for the F♮ accidentals in bars 19 and 21. The comma at the end of bar 26 means you should take a 'breath' before the next phrase starts. Do this by lifting your bow from the string at the end of the dotted minim, then landing carefully for the beginning of the next phrase. It may help to take a real breath as you do this, as if you were singing.

Jacques Offenbach (1819–80)

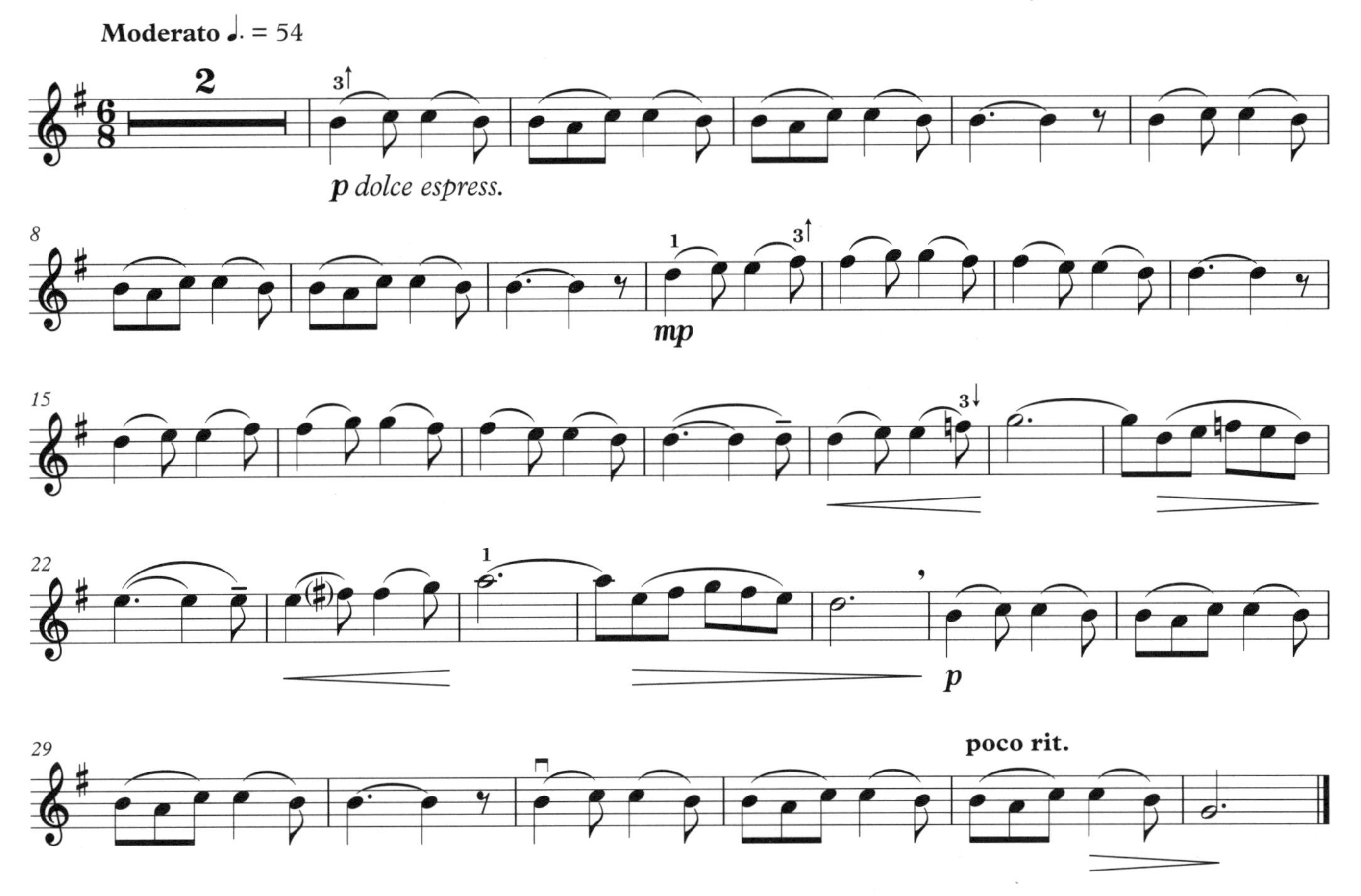

TRY...

Now try playing a two-octave C major scale in 3rd position starting on 1st-finger C on the G string. You'll need to use both high and low 3rd finger positions.

15 SHIFTING BETWEEN 1ST AND 3RD POSITION

A POSITION CHANGE, or shift, between 1st and 3rd position is simply a movement of the elbow that slides the left hand up or down the neck. The left hand moves as a unit: the thumb and 1st finger move together, the wrist stays in line with the forearm, and the side of the thumb and base of the 1st finger remain in contact with the neck. Think of your hand as moving up or down the neck on a little conveyor belt.

- A shift can be made during a gap in the music, while playing an open string, or between two stopped notes.
- The same finger or a different finger can be used for the starting and finishing notes.
- Shifts can be made on the same string or between different strings.

We usually try to make the shifting movement as quick and smooth as possible so that it doesn't disrupt the melodic line. It's important that your violin is comfortably supported on your shoulder and that your left hand is relaxed so that you can move it freely up and down the neck, so check your posture and violin position before starting each exercise and piece. You may also find it helpful to give the neck of your violin a wipe with a slightly damp cloth—a sticky neck makes shifting more difficult!

TECHNICAL TIPS

- Make sure the thumb always shifts with the hand—never leave it behind. Its position in relation to the fingers should be the same in 1st and 3rd positions.
- The shift should be made in one single movement. A common mistake is to shift in two stages, for example moving the wrist before moving the hand, or trying to reach up with the finger before moving the hand. Doing this changes your left-hand shape, making it much harder to play in tune.

Shifting during a rest or while playing an open string 

Exercise: Playing groups of notes in 1st then 3rd position

- In this exercise, each group of notes is played in 1st position, then in 3rd position. Match the tuning of the 3rd-position notes to the 1st-position notes. Play with separate bows to start with, then with slurs. Start slowly and gradually increase the tempo.
- Each shift should be made quickly, in a single smooth movement, as soon as you start playing the open string before the note in the new position. This gets your hand ready in plenty of time.
- The small guide notes are included to help you get your hand in the correct position. Start by playing them as quavers, then make them quicker as shown. When you feel confident, try leaving them out.
- Check the tuning of the 1st-finger D with the open D string after each shift.
- Check your hand and thumb position after each shift (see page 81).
- Repeat on the other strings with the same fingering.

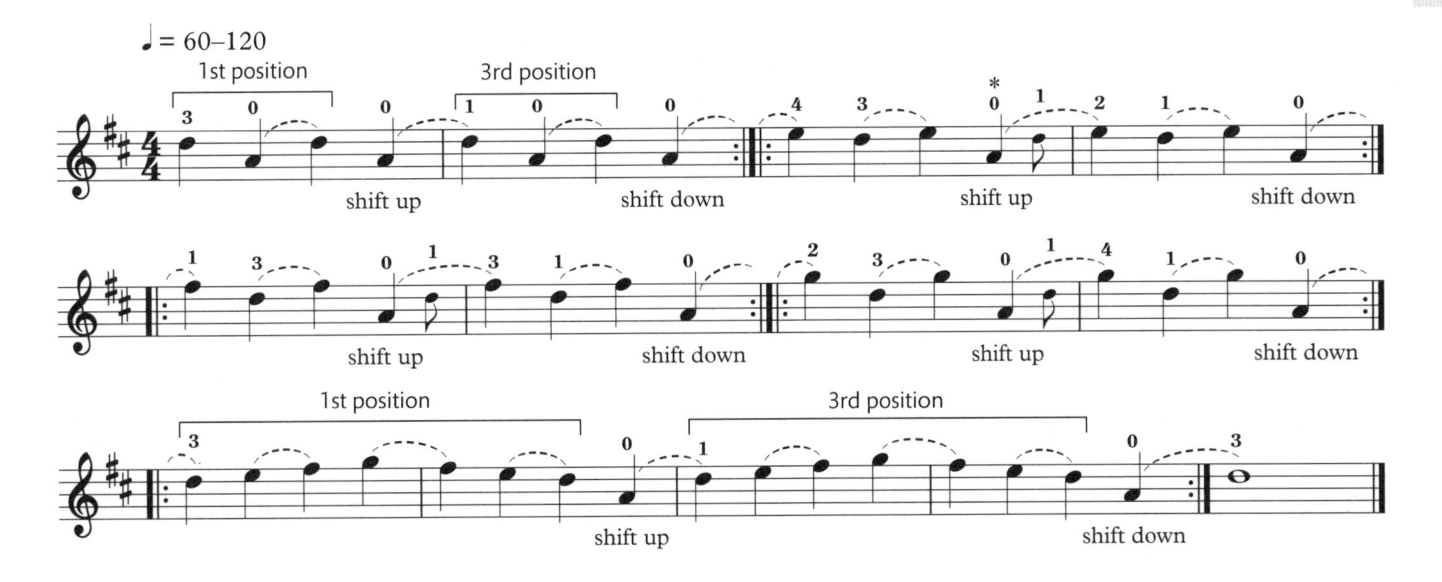

* How to play the guide notes:

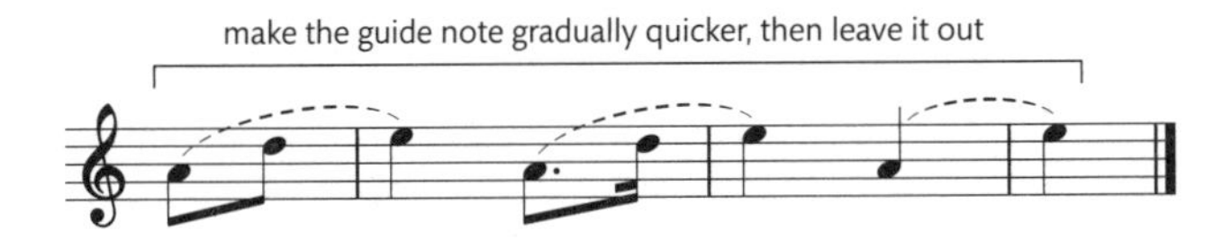

March from *Scipione*

Track 66

This piece is from Handel's opera Scipione. *Start in 3rd position. Shift down to 1st position while playing the open E in bar 2, up into 3rd position during the rest in bar 4, down to 1st position during the rest in the 2nd-time bar, and then back up into 3rd position during the rest in bar 20.*

Allemande Track 67

An Allemande is a German dance. Play the open D at the beginning with your hand ready in 3rd position. Shift down to 1st position while you play the open strings in bars 9–10, then back up to 3rd position while playing the open D at the end of the 2nd-time bar in the second section. Match the tuning of the 1st-finger Gs to the open string in the double stops. When you go back to the first section, leave out the repeat at the end of bar 8a and go straight to the 2nd-time bar.

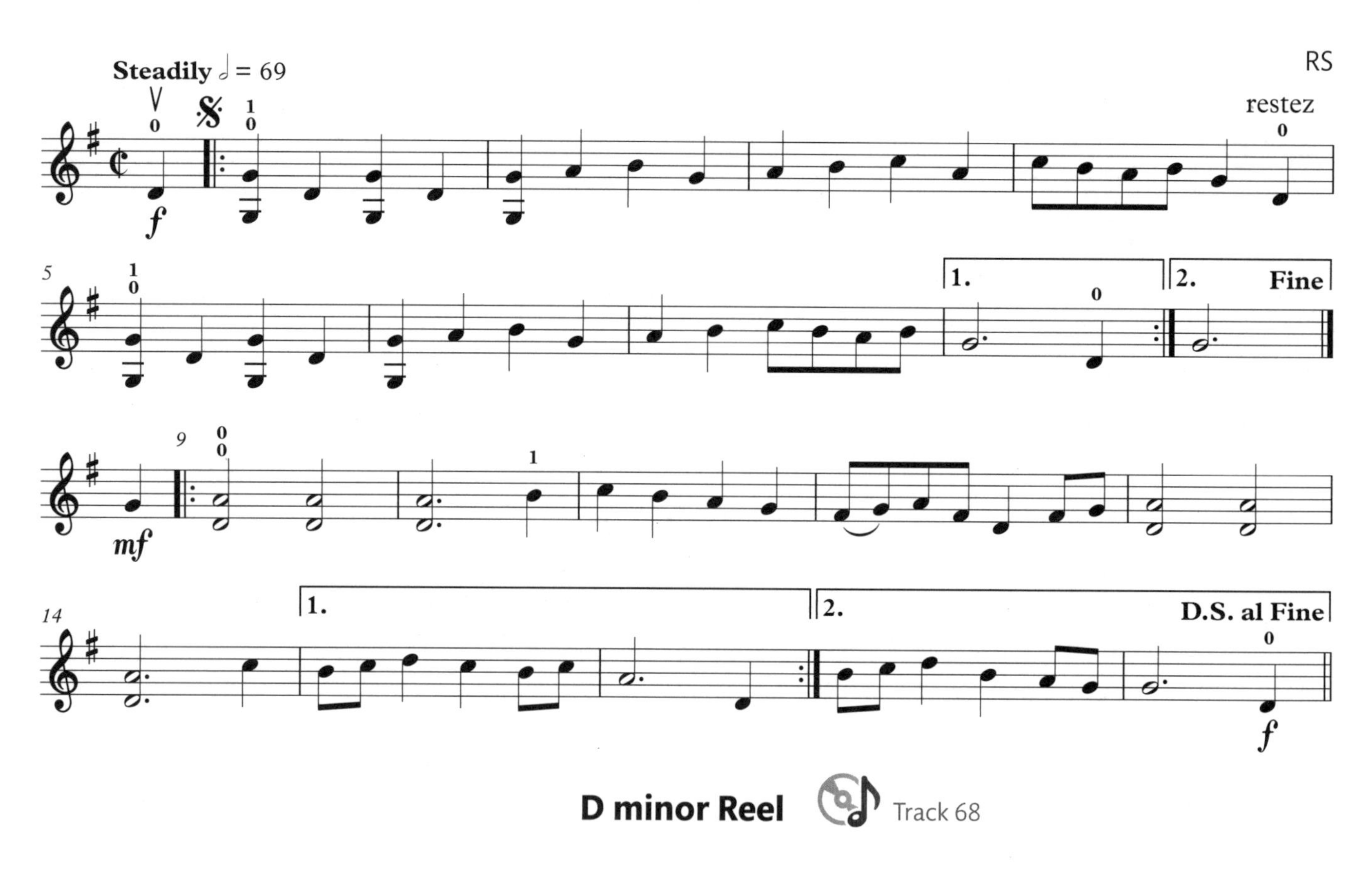

D minor Reel Track 68

Shift up to 3rd position during the rests in bars 8b and 16a, then back down to 1st position while you play the open As in bar 15.

Sevivon, Sov, Sov, Sov

Start this piece in 3rd position, then shift down to 1st position while playing the open G in bar 7b (stay in 3rd position while playing the open G in bar 7a). Watch out for the low 3rd-finger E♭s on the G string.

Israeli trad.

Shifting with one finger

- Practise this exercise one bar at a time to start with. Play each bar in 1st position, then repeat it with the shifts, as marked, and try to match the tuning.
- Start slowly, then gradually increase the tempo.
- When practising the shifts, start by start by sliding the finger quite slowly up the string so that there is an audible slide, or glissando, between the notes. Focus on moving your hand, fingers, and thumb together as a unit.
- Now try to minimize the sound of the slide by making the shift quicker, slightly reducing the pressure of the finger as it slides up the string (but don't lift it off), and very slightly (but not noticeably) lightening the bow-stroke during the shift.
- When the shifts sound really good slurred, repeat the exercise with separate bows (this is easier!). Make the shift at exactly the same time as you change bow direction so that it isn't audible.
- Keep a feeling of sensitivity in your fingertip as you shift and always 'hear' the destination note in your head. Imagine that the note is a golfing hole and your fingertip is going to land right in the middle.
- Repeat on the other strings using the same fingering.

Troubadour's Song  Track 70

In this piece you'll practise shifting up and down with your 1st finger. Try to minimize the sound of the shifts. In bar 4, shift down to 1st position while playing the open D.

RS

Tumbalalaika Track 71

This piece is a famous Russian Jewish folk song. Watch out for shifts with the 1st, 2nd, and 3rd fingers.

Russian Jewish trad.

TECHNICAL TIP

Does your violin pull away from your shoulder when you shift down? This is quite a common problem, usually caused by gripping the neck of the violin too tightly. Check that your violin is comfortably supported on your shoulder, then drop your left arm down so that it hangs loosely by your side. Adjust the position of the violin if it feels as though it might slip. Put your hand back up to the instrument, make sure you're not gripping with the thumb, and then, without the bow, slide your hand up and down the neck as if shifting. The violin shouldn't move. Now try playing the shift again.

Dans på Kolbotten

Track 72

This tune is traditionally played on the nyckelharpa, *which is a Swedish keyed fiddle. Watch out for shifts up and down with your 3rd finger. Shift down to 1st position during the open As in bars 2 and 4.*

Swedish trad. (adapted)

Shifting between different fingers

There are various ways of shifting from one finger to another. To start with we'll work on the 'basic' shift in which only one finger slides up or down the string. The shift is usually made with the starting finger (i.e. it is the starting finger that slides up or down the string), except when shifting up onto a lower finger (e.g. from 3rd up to 1st finger), in which case the shift is made with the destination finger (this avoids sliding up to a note higher than the destination note). The small guide notes in the following exercises show the movement of the shifting finger. Keep all your fingers close to the strings.

- To start with, play the following exercises slowly, with slurs, and and play the guide notes as quavers (as shown in the example below). Don't worry if you can hear a bit of a slide when you shift—just focus on staying relaxed and moving your hand up or down the neck as a unit. Aim to make the shifts in one single, easy movement, getting the guide notes exactly in tune.
- When you can do this easily, gradually make the guide notes shorter and the slides less audible until you can't hear them. This is done by making the shift quicker, reducing the pressure of the finger as it moves up the string (but don't lift it off), and very slightly (but not noticeably) lightening the bow-stroke during the shift.
- When the shifts sound really good slurred, repeat the exercises with separate bows. Make the shifts at exactly the same time as you change bow direction so that they are not audible.
- Practise the exercises in different keys, for example: G major (with C♮s instead of C♯s); C major (with C♮s and F♮s); or F major (with B♭s, C♮s, and F♮s).
- Repeat on the other strings using the same fingering.

How to practise with the guide notes:

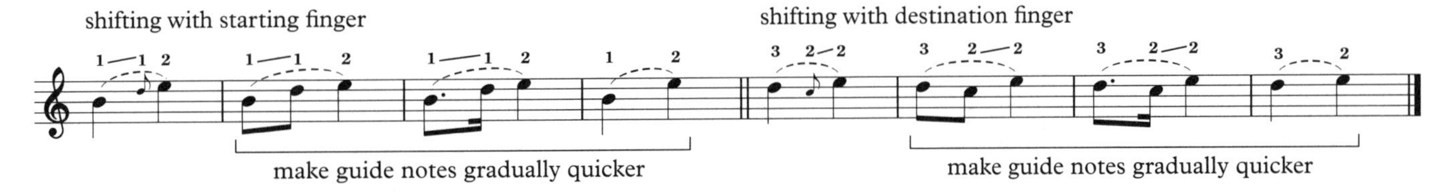

Exercise 1: Shifting from/to the 1st finger

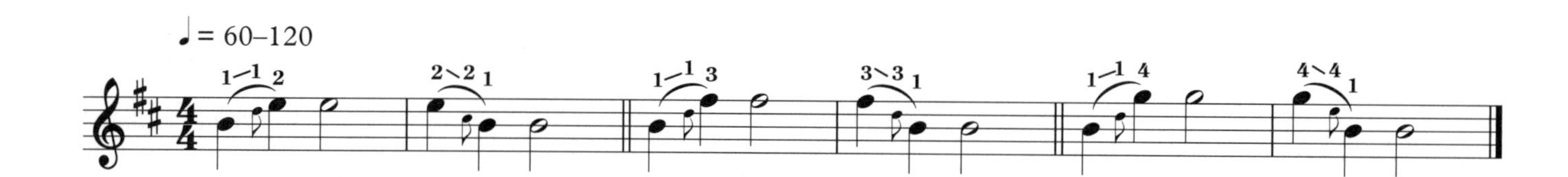

Now try playing this simple, unaccompanied melody. Aim to make the shifts as smooth and unobtrusive as possible.

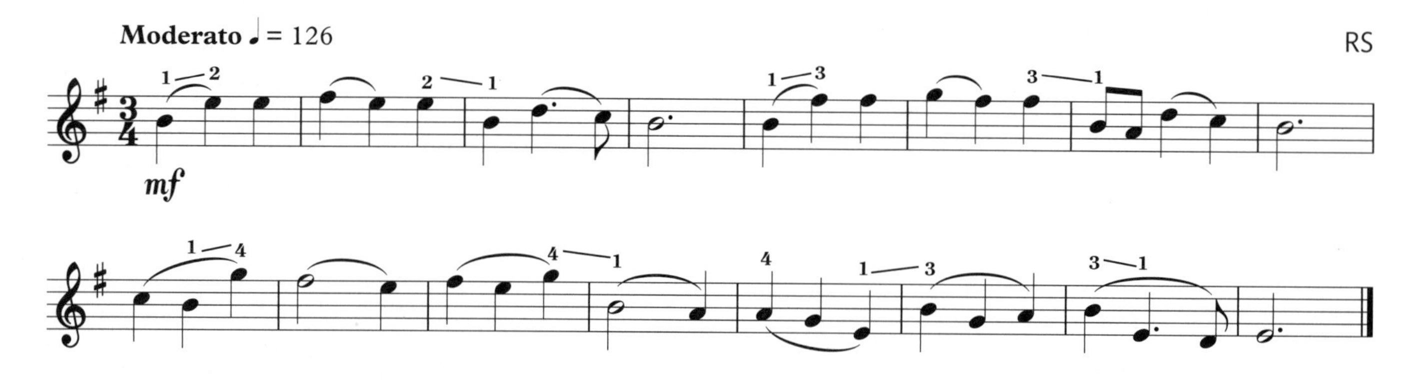

Exercise 2: Shifting from/to the 2nd finger

Exercise 3: Shifting from/to the 3rd finger

* Note: these upward shifts (from a higher to a lower finger) are made with the 'destination' finger.

The next pieces include the various different types of shift that you've learnt in this chapter. Only the fingering for the destination finger of any shift will be given from now on; if in doubt as to how to make the shift, refer back to the exercises above.

Hungarian Dance No. 13

Track 73

Play the harmonic in the last bar of the Vivace section by extending your 4th finger while in 3rd position—you shouldn't need to shift or change your thumb position to reach it.

Johannes Brahms (1833-97)

TECHNICAL TIP

Work on shifts in your pieces by:

- Including the notes before and after the shift rather than just practising the shift on its own.
- Practising shifts in both directions (up and down).
- Practising shifts with slurs even if they're not slurred in the piece—it's easy to hide a poor shift with a bow change!

5/4 time signature

A 5/4 time signature means you should count five crotchet beats per bar. The beats are often divided into a group of three notes followed by a group of two notes: ***one***, two, three, ***four***, five.

Soupa Mana

Before you play this piece, practise clapping crotchets along to your metronome, emphasizing the first of every five beats. Then clap the 5/4 pulse again, this time emphasizing the first and fourth beats.

Greek trad.

TRY...

Now try adding shifts to pieces that you played earlier in the book. Try, for example: 'A Csitari Hegyek Alatt' (page 28, the second line would sound good in 3rd position), and 'Ballade' (page 58, the end of bar 10 to the beginning bar 22 would sound good in 3rd position).

Alabama Sunset

Track 75

Look out for the minor 3rd interval between your 1st and 2nd fingers in bars 2 and 34, and for the augmented 2nd interval between your 1st and 2nd fingers in bars 23–4 (a minor 3rd interval and an augmented 2nd interval are the same size—three semitones—but are spelt differently). Make sure you reach far enough with your fingers to get these intervals in tune.

RS

Sliding shifts

Usually we try to minimize slides when shifting, but they can be used expressively, particularly in jazz-influenced music. At the end of bar 31 of 'Bourbon Street Stomp' there is a slide from 1st-position C♯ up to 3rd-position F♯ on the A string. This is done by making an audible shift up with the 3rd finger. Start by playing a glissando from 3rd-finger D to F♯, as shown below. Gradually make the D shorter in duration and reduce the pressure of the 3rd finger on the string at the very beginning of the slide so that there isn't an obvious starting note. The 4th-finger slide up to the final note of the piece is easier: the movement is the same as a shift, but with an audible slide—start the slide when you change bow direction. The other slides in the piece are played in 1st position as described on page 70.

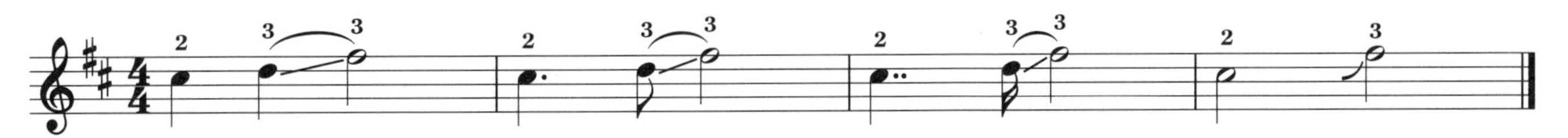

Bourbon Street Stomp   Track 76

This piece should be played with swing quavers. Look out for accidentals and sliding semitones, and see 'Sliding shifts' above for advice on playing the slides.

RS

Breton Mariner's Song

The fingering shown in bars 14–16a of this piece involves a shift down to 1st position, but a more musical fingering would be to stay in 3rd position for the whole phrase, playing the F♯s with the 4th finger on the G string. This requires you to reach up a semitone higher with your 4th finger than you are used to—see if you can do it.

Two-octave D major scale and arpeggio

- The **key-signature** of D major is **two sharps**: **F♯** and **C♯**.
- Shift into 3rd position where marked, moving your whole hand up the neck as a unit.
- Take care not to leave your thumb behind when shifting.
- Play the scale with even notes as well as with the 'long tonic' rhythm shown below.

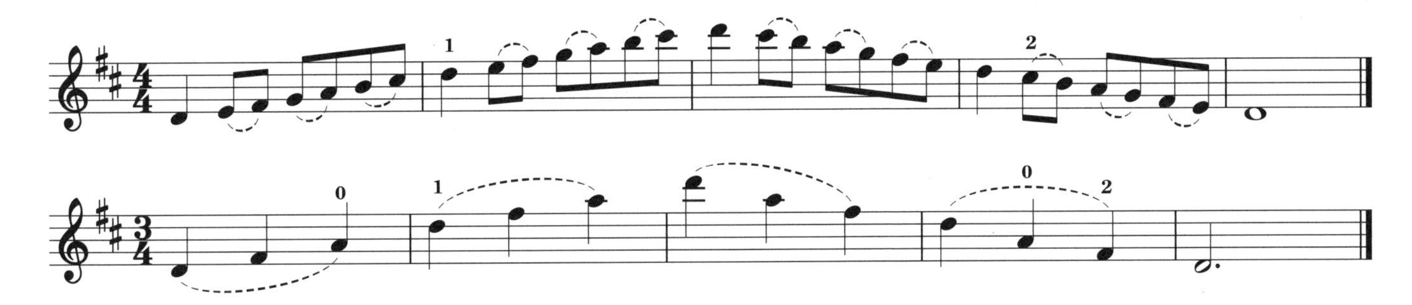

APPENDIX: THE CIRCLE OF 5THS

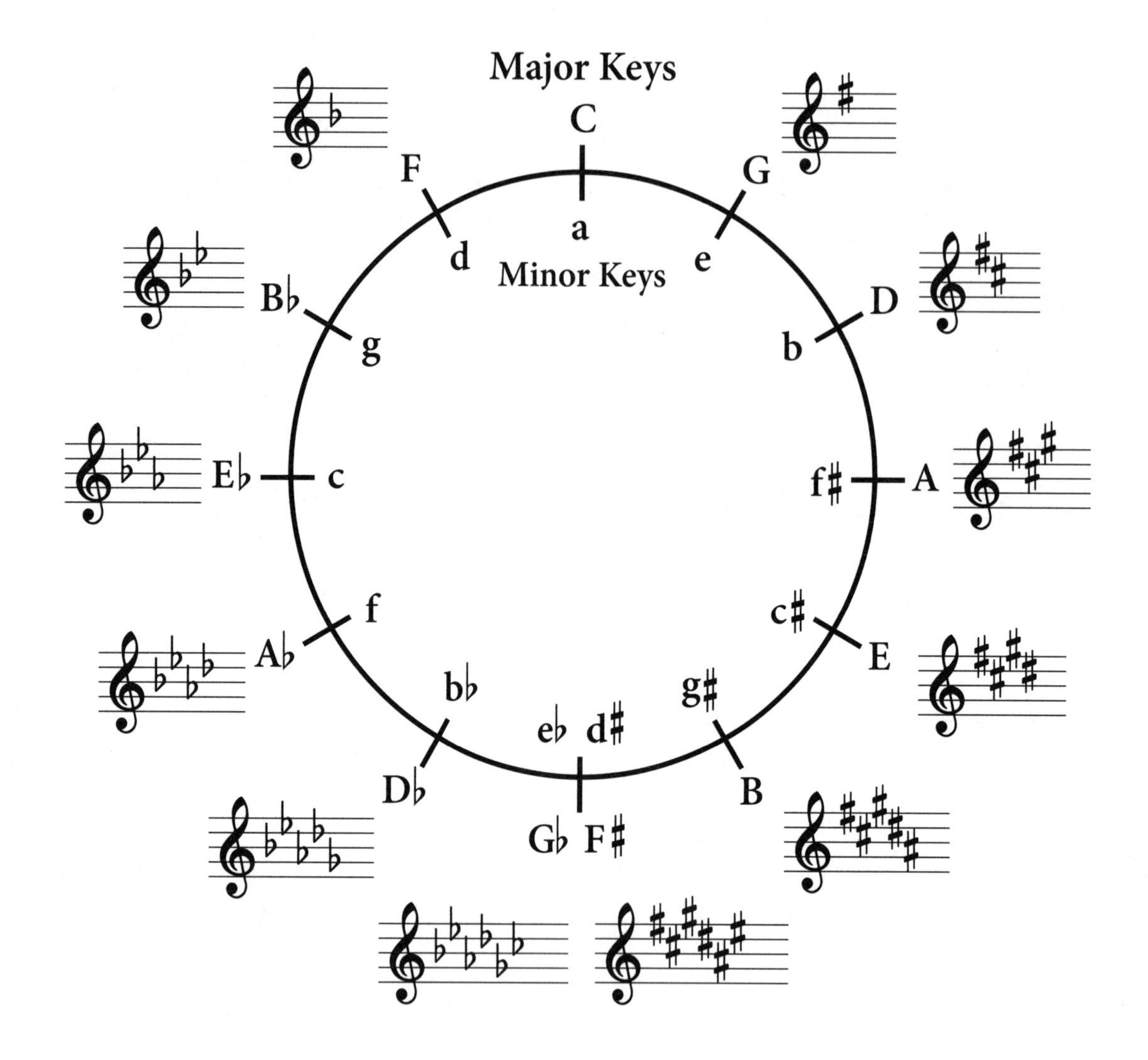

- This circle of 5ths diagram shows the twelve most commonly used major and relative minor scales and their key signatures. It is so called because the key signatures are listed a perfect 5th apart (a perfect 5th is equal to seven semitones). Keys a perfect 5th apart always differ by one sharp or flat.
- The notes ascend by 5ths as we move clockwise around the circle, giving us the sharp key signatures. The key of C is at the top, with no sharps or flats in its key signature. Count five notes up from C and we arrive at G (C–D–E–F–G), which has one sharp in its key signature. Count up another five notes to D and another sharp is added to the key signature, and so on.
- The notes descend by 5ths as we move anti-clockwise around the circle, giving us the flat key signatures. A 5th below C is F (C–B–A–G–F), which has one flat in its key signature. Likewise, a 5th below F is B♭, which has two flats in its key signature, and so on.
- The order of the sharps or flats in a key signature also follows the circle of 5ths. For example, the key signature of A major is F♯–C♯–G♯ (clockwise around the circle of 5ths), and the key signature of E♭ major is B♭–E♭–A♭ (anti-clockwise around the circle of 5ths starting from B♭).